THE KUNSTHISTORISCHES MUSEUM

IN VIENNA

A Picture Panorama

*Published in
collaboration with the
Kunsthistorisches Museum in Vienna*

Editor:
Georg Kugler

BONECHI VERLAG STYRIA

*Vertrieb
für Österreich*
VERLAG STYRIA
Schönaugasse 64
A-8010 GRAZ

für Deutschland
AZN
Hooge Weg 71
D-47623 Kevelaer

für die Schweiz
Herder AG Basel
Muttenzerstraße 109
CH-4133 Pratteln 1

THE KUNSTHISTORISCHES MUSEUM IN VIENNA

Publication created and designed by Casa Editrice Bonechi
Project and graphic realization: Sonia Gottardo
Videolayout: "m&m", Florence
Editing: Anna Baldini

Text: Georg Kugler

Translation: Erika Pauli *for* Studio Comunicare, Florence

© Copyright
CASA EDITRICE BONECHI
Via Cairoli 18/b
I-50131 Florence

Printed in Italy by the Centro Stampa Editoriale Bonechi.

*The cover, layout and artwork by the Casa Editrice Bonechi
graphic artists in this publication are protected
by international copyright.*

*The illustrations are from the photographic fund of the
Kunsthistorisches Museum in Vienna* (photographs Kitlitschka,
Erich Lessing, Ali Meyer, Udo Otto)

ISBN 3 222 12398 5

* * *

CONTENTS

INTRODUCTION

Theseus and the Centaur by Antonio Canova.

*T*he "Kunsthistorisches Museum" (Museum of the History of Art) houses art that originally comprised the private collections of the Austrian royal family. Emperors, kings, archdukes and archduchesses of the House of Hapsburg began to take a personal interest in collecting in the 15th century, with widely varying results. Some of them, however, collected systematically in grand style so that today the Hapsburg collections of Vienna and Madrid rank among the most important in the world. In the 16th and 17th centuries the Hapsburgs held dominion over almost all of central and southern Europe, as well as the Netherlands to the west. The political importance of the dynasty is reflected in the wealth of its artistic heritage. Three collectors played a fundamental role in the formation of what is now the "Kunsthistorisches Museum", and merit a brief introduction. The interests of Archduke Ferdinand II were primarily historical. Governor of Bohemia between 1547 and 1563, prince of the Tyrol and the bordering regions from 1564 to 1595, he installed his collections in Schloss Ambras near Innsbruck in line with a true museum criteria. His nephew, Emperor Rudolf II, of a more universal and artistic mind, concentrated his "Kunstkammer" (Cabinet of Art) and his picture gallery in the fortress-castle Hradschin of Prague. But the title of founder of the picture gallery in Vienna unquestionably belongs to Archduke Leopold William who, as Spanish governor of the Netherlands between 1647 and 1656, was in a position to buy important paintings in Brussels, then an important center of the art market. He later transferred these paintings to Vienna where they were inherited in 1662 by the emperor, Leopold I. Numerous members of the Hapsburg family played a part in enriching the Vienna collections, at times as patrons of contemporary artists. Albrecht Dürer worked for Emperor Maximilian I, Titian, Arcimboldo and Giambologna for Emperor Maximilian II. Hans von Aachen, Bartolomäus Spranger and Adrian de Fries for Emperor Rudolf II. David Teniers painted in the service of Archduke Leopold William, Velázquez for King Philip V of Spain, Pompeo Batoni and Bernardo Bellotto for the Empress Maria Theresa.

The name "Kunsthistorisches Museum" does not date back to the origins of these collections but first appeared with reference to the magnificent building erected in Vienna between 1871 and 1891 so that the long extant collections could be exhibited together in a distinguished and scientifically organized installation. Although the imperial collections were accessible to the public prior to 1891, they were dispersed in various places. The imperial picture gallery was housed in the buildings of the castle of the Upper Belvedere, while the collections of ancient art - Egyptian, Near Eastern, Greek and Roman - were concentrated in the Lower Belvedere. So-called minor works of art, dating to the Baroque, were on exhibit in other rooms, side by side with Renaissance objects of the decorative arts - goldwork, bronzes and ivories, in part from the famous collection in Schloss Ambras. Numerous other masterpieces of the decorative arts, including the insignia of the Golden Fleece and the Hapsburg family jewels, were kept in the Schatzkammer (Treasury) in the Hofburg. Portions of the present collection of antique art, together with coins and medals, were also kept in other rooms of the Hofburg and were accessible to the public as a museum. The collections of minerals, shells and other wonders of nature to be found in adjacent rooms, are now to be seen in the "Naturhistorisches Museum" (Natural History Museum). Set directly across from the "Kunsthistorisches Museum" and absolutely identical in shape and size from the outside, this building was built to bring together the Hapsburg collections of natural history and anthropology, which up to 1881 had been dispersed in various sites. The different collections had been rearranged in the Kunsthistorisches Museum even prior to its official inauguration in 1891 by Emperor Francis Joseph. Initially the Arms Cabinet, with armor and weapons, formerly on exhibit as a monument to Austrian military glory in the Arsenal where the great Heeresgeschichtliches Museum (Historical Army Museum) is still to be found, was installed here. Fifty years after being moved to the new museum, the collection was once more transferred to make room for a more modern exhibition of the minor art objects. Today it is housed in the rooms known as the Hofkammer (Court Cabinet), Jagdkammer (Hunting Cabinet) and Rustkammer (Armory Cabinet) open to the public on the second floor of the Neue Burg, a wing added to the original Hofburg. The latter houses the collections of ancient musical instruments, the Ephesos Museum and other collections which, like those of the Stallburg, Schloss Schönbrunn and Schloss Ambras (near Innsbruck), are, even though situated elsewhere, part of the collective patrimony of the Kunsthistorisches Museum. Only the collections in the main building overlooking the Ring are presented in this book, with illustrations of the most important paintings in the Gallery, together with a few selected examples of pieces in the Egyptian-Near Eastern Collection, the Collection of Antiquities and the Kunstkammer.

THE PICTURE GALLERY (DIE GEMÄLDEGALERIE)

*A*ll the collections of the Kunsthistorisches Museum, including the Picture Gallery, have their own strengths and weaknesses. These reflect the personal tastes and interests of the collectors of past centuries, when no attempt was made to illustrate the history of art. The concept of an encyclopedic approach was developed in the 18th century and eventually led to the creation of the 19th century educational museum. By then the Hapsburg collections were already basically what they are today. Even now the nature of the Picture Gallery of the Kunsthistorisches Museum is that of a private royal collection. The strong points, such as the large number of Netherlandish, Flemish, and Venetian paintings, still strike the eye today as much as the deficiencies, of which the almost complete absence of French and English painting is a good example.

Royal collecting activity turned to painting as such at a relatively late date, and what mattered most was the content and subject of the picture. It is therefore no surprise that what they were primarily interested in was portraits. After all, at the beginning of the 16th century, antique coins were collected because they showed imperial portraits. The first great collector of the house of Hapsburg, Archduke Ferdinand II, who initially resided in Prague and then, from 1566 on, in Innsbruck, collected almost exclusively portraits and a few paintings of historical events. Only a few of the more than one thousand paintings still to be found in his "Ambras" collection are of interest as art from the present-day point of view. Emperor Rudolf II was the first collector whose interests went beyond historic testimonials and family politics, and who was attracted by art for art's sake, with a concern for the artists whom he admired and honored. In Prague Rudolf II put together a comprehensive collection of works of art and natural curiosities (Kunst- und Wunderkammer or Cabinet of Art and Marvels) which became legendary even in his time. Stll today the Kunsthistorisches Museum possesses world-famous objects from this highly varied collection. His picture gallery was not only extensive but was, above all, of high artistic quality. His centered his attention on the Italian and German Renaissance, especially the works of Albrecht Dürer. Rudolf II was a passionate collector and pursued his aims with extraordinary tenacity. In the last month of the Thirty Years' War (1648), the Emperor's picture gallery was plundered by Swedish troops and later, when the collection of the Swedish royal house was sold, the paintings were scattered to the four winds. Some of the more important works, including paintings by Correggio, Parmigianino, Dürer, and Bruegel, had been taken to Vienna after the Emperor's death, where, except for a few which returned to Prague, they remained. Later emperors once more built up the picture gallery of this city: Emperor Ferdinand III, for example, obtained Titian's Ecce Homo and Rubens' Banquet of Venus for Prague. When the imperial picture gallery was reorganized in the 18th century, these works greatly enhanced the collection. The collectors of past times almost always showed interest in contemporary art, and Rudolf II collected paintings by Dutch and German artists, some of whom he called to Prague as court painters so that reference came to be made to a Rudolfian school of painting. The most prominent masters included Hans von Aachen, Joseph Heintz, Bartolomäus Spranger. The works of these artists form a characteristic ensemble of the Vienna Gallery.

Just as important for the development of the Vienna Gallery as the masterpieces collected by Rudolf is the family tradition. Art collecting and art patronage were considered a duty, to which the relationship between Charles V and Titian on the one hand, and Rudolf's passion for collecting on the other bear witness. After all, not even the scientifically trained curators of the 19th and 20th centuries succeeded in freeing themselves from this tradition.

Archduke Leopold William, a grandnephew of Rudolf II, who received the office of Statolder (governor) in the Netherlands in 1647, must be credited as the real founder of the royal Picture Gallery. In Brussels he built up his own gallery as well as buying paintings for his brother, Emperor Ferdinand II, and his castle in Prague. His income as governor, as Grand Master of the Teutonic Order, and the proceeds from his several bishoprics, all favored his purchases, as did the political situation at the end of the Thirty Years' War and the revolution in England. After the fall of Charles I of England, Oliver Cromwell had the Royal Gallery collection and that of the Duke of Buckingham put up for auction in Antwerp, and a large part of this stock of exceptional paintings was acquired by Leopold William. His collection was comprehensively inventoried and represented in paintings by David Teniers the Younger. At the end of his term as governor, it was moved from Brussels to Vienna and then left as a bequest to his nephew, Emperor Leopold I. The Vienna Gallery's rich store of works by the Venetians, such as Titian, Giorgione, the two Palmas, Veronese and Tintoretto, as well as panels by the earlier Netherland painters, Van Eyck, Hugo van der Goes, and Rogier van der Weyden, all come from the gallery of Archduke Leopold William.

Of works by contemporary masters, the Archduke naturally favored those by his court painter and gallery director Teniers, as well as those by the greatest of all Flemish artists, Rubens, who had recently died, and his pupils. He may personally have ordered the great Feast of the Bean King from Jordaens.

In the Baroque period, during which the systematic and representative collecting of paintings and other works of art was increasingly pursued, politics - primarily family politics of the

Gustav Klimt. Egyptian Art (between the columns on the left) and Ancient Italian Art (in the spandrels) on the east wall of the staircase of the Kunsthistorisches Museum.

Julius Viktor Berger. Artists around Emperor Charles V, including, at the center, Benvenuto Cellini with his "Saltcellar". Detail of the painting The Patrons of the House of Hapsburg on the ceiling of room XIX on the mezzanine of the Kunsthistorisches Museum.

royal family - contributed to significant acquisitions. The countless portraits of Spanish relatives of all generations, beginning with Charles V, came to Vienna for family reasons - not even the masterful portraits of the Infanta by Velázquez were sent there purely as works of art.

The Baroque spirit led to an incorporation and a subordination of paintings and sculpture, and even of books, to their architectural setting. The result under Emperor Charles VI was a complete rearrangement of the gallery in which the principal aim was the allover effect of a decoratively arranged wall of paintings. A painted inventory picture gives us an idea of what it loked like. Many a masterpiece which we admire in the Gallery today appeared for the first time in 1730 - for example, Holbein's portrait of Jane Seymour and Rembrandt's portrait of his son Titus reading.

The next generation had already outgrown this magnificent but static presentation of works of art. Adhering to the spirit of the Enlightenment, Maria Theresa and her son Joseph II decided to open the art treasures to the public and therefore to reconstruct the exhibits on educational principles. Since the large, in part gigantic, altarpieces by Rubens, Van Dyck and Caravaggio, which these sovereigns had collected, could not be fitted into the gallery, it was decided in 1776 to transfer the collection to the Belvedere, the former garden palace of Eugene Prince of Savoy. Not until 1781, when a foreign expert, Christian van Mechel of Basle, was called in, was the installation terminated, and in 1783 the first catalogue was published. Now for the first time the great gaps in the picture collection became evident. To close these gaps attempts were made to trade with the galleries in Florence, governed at the time by the Hapsburg and Lorraine families. Important additions were unfortunately outweighed by later losses. Due to the events of the Napoleonic wars, these compensatory exchanges were never completed. Not only that, but forty of the more than 400 paintings carried away to Paris by the French troops were never returned.

Emperor Francis I of Austria, who reigned in the first third of the 19th century, increased the painting collection in a rather haphazard manner, usually by fortuitous rather than systematic purchases and missed many opportunities. The only collection enlarged was that of Dutch interiors and landscapes. Among the acquisitions was the incomparable masterpiece by Ruisdael, The Forest. But greater interest and attention was devoted to objects of antique art and prehistory. It was in those years that the fortuitously discovered gold treasures of the Barbarian Migrations, which are such a great attraction of the Vienna Antikensammlung, entered the royal collections.

In closing it should be pointed out that in 1918 the Vienna Gallery, as was the case with all other Hapsburg art collections, was expropriated and became state property. It still however adheres to the traditions and does all in its power to meet the demands placed upon a modern public museum. The constant advance of scientific studies and the well designed presentation of the objects in the immutable setting of the magnificent building bear witness to this commitment. In line with this aim was the installation in 1967 of a second gallery housing works that may not appeal to the public at large in an initial visit. The greater and lesser acquisitions of the past decade fit well into the present collection and have also extended it in a specific direction. Masters of the Danubian school (Cranach, Altdorfer, Huber) are now represented in the Gallery by important panels, thanks to continuous purchases from the 1920's on. The international rank of the Vienna Gallery has at the same time been maintained with the acquisition of masterpieces such as Dürer's Portrait of a Young Venetian Woman and Vermeer's Allegory of Painting.

ROGIER VAN DER WEYDEN

(Tournai 1399 or 1400 - Brussels 1464)

Crucifixion Triptych

The central panel shows Christ on the cross with Mary and John on the left. On the right a pair of unidentified patrons. On the wings, St. Mary Magdalen (left) and St. Veronica.

Oak,
central panel 96 x 69 cm
wings 101 x 35 cm each
ca. 1440/45

Rogier van der Weyden was exceedingly active in Brussels. The expressive power of his paintings shows him still bound to the late Gothic tradition; however, like the brothers Jan and Hubert van Eyck, he too attempted to depict the full range of reality. This intention is favored by his pictorial technique, based on extraordinarily luminous colors. Rogier's paintings were appreciated not only by his contemporaries but also by the early collectors of Flemish panel painting and excercised a strong influence on the painting of central Europe. Rogier's *Crucifixion Triptych*, like the works of Jan van Eyck and Hans Memling, was acquired by Archduke Leopold William around 1650 and therefore was part of the patrimony of the Viennese Gallery from its very beginnings.

JOOS VAN CLEVE
(Cleve ca. 1485 - Antwerp 1540)

Virgin and Child

oak panel, 74 x 56 cm
ca. 1530

This type of devotional image was very widespread and it is therefore thought to have originally been painted for a small private altar.

JAN VAN EYCK
(Maastricht ca. 1390 - Bruges 1441)

Portrait of Cardinal Nicola Albergati
(1375-1443)

oak panel, 34 x 27 cm
ca. 1435

In 1431 the Cardinal was papal legate at the Burgundian court in Dijon, with the task of mediating peace between the hostile French parties. Philip the Good, Duke of Burgundy, whose role in these disputes was decisive, evidently commissioned his court painter Jan van Eyck to paint a portrait of the legate. The artist proved himself to be a master portrait painter, combining unqualified faithfulness to nature and keen observation with dignity and monumentality.

HUGO VAN DER GOES
(ca. 1410 - Monastery of Rodenale near Brussels 1482)

Altar diptych with the Fall of Man and Lamentation over the Dead Christ

two oak panels, 33 x 22 cm (The Fall of Man)*, 34 x 23 cm* (Lamentation over the Dead Christ)
before 1475

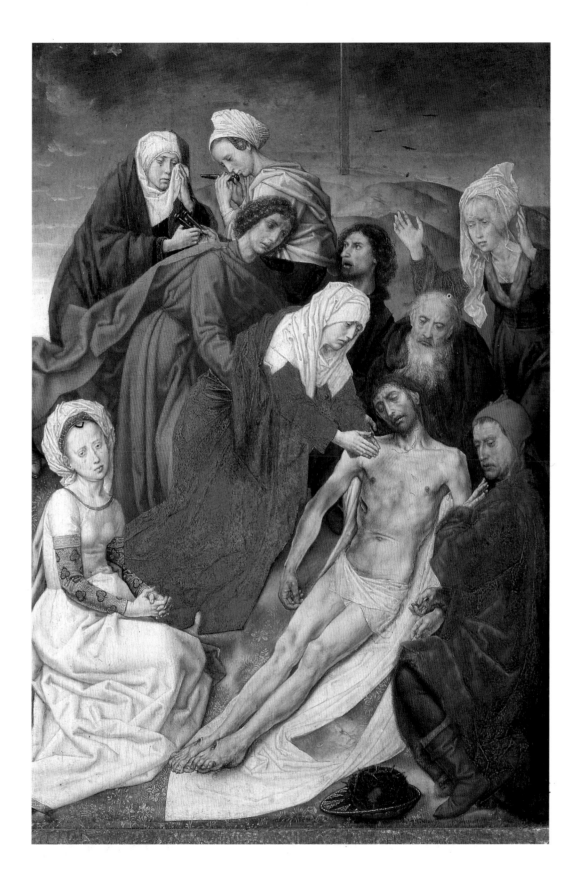

In these two scenes the painter illustrates the theme of the fall of man and the redemption of mankind by means of the crucifixion of Christ. The first of these subjects, in particular, is handled in an innovative manner, depicting Eden and the first human couple in a highly naturalistic way. The spatial perspective in the landscape of the terrestrial paradise is also very modern, while in the Lamentation it still depends on the Late Gothic tradition.

HIERONYMUS BOSCH
(ca. 1450 - s'Hertogenbosch 1516)

Child with a Pinwheel

oak panel, 57 x 32 cm
ca. 1480

The painting is on the back of a small shutter of a triptych with Christ bearing the cross. The picture of the child with a walker and pinwheel is an allegory of ignorance and stupidity alluding to the passion of Christ. An interpretation of the figure as that of the Christ Child is unfounded.

JOACHIM PATINIER
(ca. 1485 - Antwerp 1524)

The Baptism of Christ

oak panel, 60 x 76.5 cm
ca. 1515

The Baptism of Christ in the river Jordan which was so often represented is here set into the midst of what might be called a "cosmic" landscape. His stress on the importance of landscape makes Patinier the founder of a tradition that leads to Bruegel and Dürer.

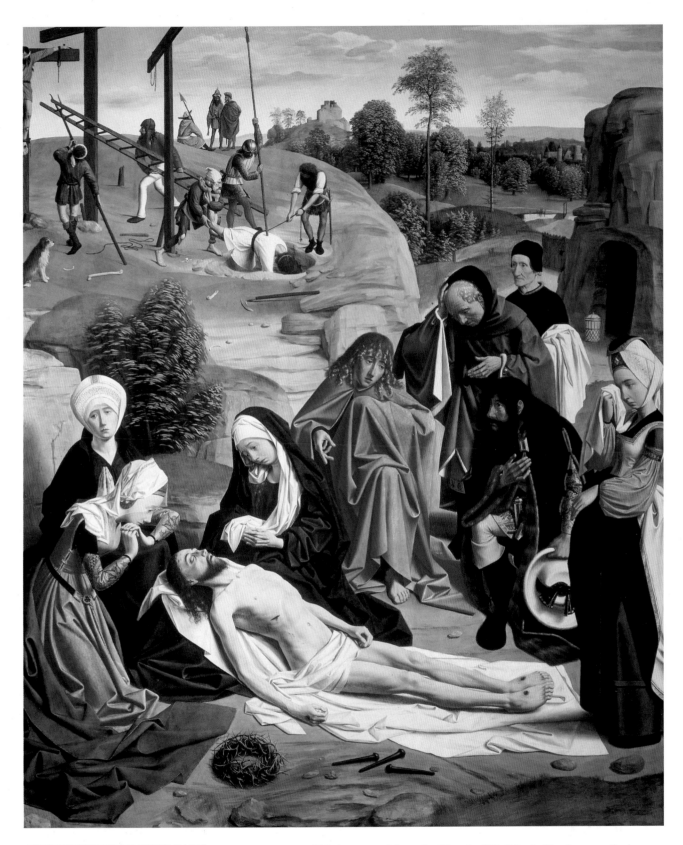

GEERTGEN TOT SINT JANS

(ca. 1460 - Haarlem after 1490)

Mourning over the Dead Christ

oak panel, 175 x 139 cm
ca. 1485

This large panel from the Church of St. John in Haarlem was the inner side of the shutter of a triptych, the outer side of which is also in the Vienna Gallery. The triptych was later destroyed, except for these two paintings, and this panel was given to Charles I, king of England. After the fall of the monarchy, the painting was bought by Archduke Leopold William in 1648 at the auction of the Duke of Hamilton's collection.

LUCAS CRANACH THE ELDER

(Kronach 1472 - Weimar 1553)

St. Jerome Penitent

linden panel, 55.5 x 41.5 cm
ca. 1502

This picture is the first dated painting by Cranach, founder of the so-called Danubian School. In the period between 1500 and 1504 the painter was active in Vienna and other cities in Austria and Bavaria. His early works are filled with a youthful emotional power and great religious expressiveness.

ALBRECHT DÜRER

(Nürnberg 1471 - 1528)

The Adoration of the Trinity

poplar panel, 135 x 123 cm
1511

The large altarpiece with the representation of the Trinity which floats over the assembly of saints and Christians is one of Dürer's principal works and one of the outstanding works of art in the Vienna Gallery. This painting, in which Albrecht Dürer offers us a synthesis of his art and his creed, was commissioned by a burgher of Nürnberg, Matthaeus Landauer, for the chapel in the "Zwölfbrüderhaus" which he had endowed in 1511. The donor can be recognized as the old man on the left and his son-in-law as the knight in goldern armor on the right. Dürer also portrayed himself in the terrestrial spring landscape, under the heavenly vision. He stands next to a panel which proudly proclaims: "Albertus Dürer Noricus Faciebat Anno A Virginis Partu 1511."

ALBRECHT ALTDORFER
(Regensburg ? ca. 1480 - Regensburg 1538)

The Entombment and the Resurrection of Christ

both panels spruce, each 70 x 37 cm
1518

Albrecht Altdorfer was the second great master of the
Danubian School. His works move away from the classical
Renaissance style in their expressive power and exuberance of
feeling. The two panels with the *Entombment* and the
Resurrection are the side panels of the predella of a large
polyptych painted for the Augustinian Monastery of St. Florian
in Upper Austria. Two large panels with the *Passion of Christ*
and the *Legend of St. Sebastian* still remain in St. Florian.

ALBRECHT DÜRER ▶
(Nürnberg 1471 - 1528)

The Virgin and Child with a Sliced Pear

linden panel, 49 x 37 cm
1512

Among the countless representations of the Madonna and Child
in German painting, special importance, both art historically
and as a popular painting, can be assigned to Dürer's so-called
"Blue Madonna". In 1512 when Dürer painted this picture, he
was still completely under the influence of the Italian
Renaissance painters, as is evident from the movement and
powerful plasticity of the body of the Christ Child. On the
other hand, Dürer once more also reveals his mastery of
drawing, which is precise and faithful to nature in every detail.
Both Dürer's *Adoration of the Trinity* and the *Blue Madonna*
were acquired by Emperor Rudolf.

ALBRECHT DÜRER
(Nürnberg 1471 - 1528)

Portrait of Johann Kleeberger
(Nürnberg 1486 - Lyons 1547)

linden panel, 36.5 x 36.5 cm
1526

During his extraordinarily eventful life, Kleeberger, also known
as "the good German", acquired a large patrimony which he
then distributed to the poor of Lyons. Dürer painted his portrait
in the form of a medal. The head looks like a marble bust but
has an extraordinarily alert expression. Dürer's monogram and
the date are in the upper right hand corner, while the zodiac
sign of Leo and the sitter's coat of arms are in the other
corners.

ALBRECHT DÜRER
(Nürnberg 1471 - 1528)

Portrait of the Emperor Maximilian I
(Neustadt, Vienna 1459 - Wels 1519)

linden panel, 74 x 61.5 cm
1519

For over a decade Albrecht Dürer was in the service of the
Emperor Maximilian, who commissioned woodcuts,
illustrations for the books he himself published, from the
painter. The portrait was not commissioned until the
sovereign's last year and Dürer made the preparatory drawing
in June of 1518 in Augsburg. The portrait was finished after the
death of his patron and the solemn inscription at the top
proclaims the emperor's glory to posterity as well as giving us
his birth and death dates.

POTENTISSIMVS · MAXIMVS · ET · INVICTISSIMVS · CÆSAR · MAXIMILIANVS
QVI · CVNCTOS · SVI · TEMPORIS · REGES · ET · PRINCIPES · IVSTICIA · PRVDENCIA
MAGNANIMITATE · LIBERALITATE · PRÆCIPVE · VERO · BELLICA · LAVDE · ET
ANIMI · FORTIDVDINE · SVPERAVIT · NATVS · EST · ANNO · SALVTIS · HVMANÆ
M · CCCC · LIX · DIE · MARCII · IX · VIXIT · ANNOS · LIX · MENSES · IX · DIES · XXV
DECESSIT · VERO · ANNO · M · D · XIX · MENSIS · IANVARII · DIE · XII · QVEM · DEVS
OPT · MAX · IN · NVMERVM · VIVENCIVM · REFERRE · VELIT ·

**HANS HOLBEIN
THE YOUNGER**

(Augsburg 1497 - London 1543)

Portrait of a Young Merchant

oak panel, 46.5 x 35 cm
1541

20

**HANS HOLBEIN
THE YOUNGER**

(Augsburg 1497 - London 1543)

Jane Seymour, Queen of England

oak panel, 65.4 x 40.7 cm
1536

In the beginning Holbein, who painted the two portraits on the preceding pages, studied with his father, Hans the Elder, in Augsburg. From there he wandered to Basle and in 1532 to London. No less a person than Erasmus of Rotterdam recommended him to Sir Thomas More. He soon entered the service of King Henry VIII and became world famous as the portrait painter of the English court. The Vienna Gallery owns an unusually large and important group of seven portraits by

Holbein, all of which originated in London. At the time, the
city was the center of the international market, so the presence
of the young German merchant who asked his fellow
countryman, the painter, to paint his portrait is not difficult to
explain. Jane Seymour became the King's third wife in 1536
and had been a lady-in-waiting to her immediate predecessors.
A few months later she died. Like Van Eyck and Dürer,
Holbein proved himself a master in the art of portraiture, for
despite a precise representation of all details, especially the
clothing, he did not neglect the overall impression of the
subject and thus achieved a true-to-life quality in his portraits
as perhaps no other painter after him.

◀ ANTHONIS MOR VAN DASHORST
(Utrecht 1517 - Antwerp 1576)

Portrait of Antoine Perrenot de Granvelle
(Besançon 1517 - Madrid 1585)

oak panel, 107 x 82 cm
1549

While Mor's role as an outstanding Dutch portrait painter was
important, so was his lasting influence on Spanish portraiture
as court painter to Philip II in Madrid and Lisbon. The portrait
of Granvelle dates to the year 1549 when he
was still bishop of Arras and when he had not yet begun
his great political career in the service of Charles V and
Margaret of Parma.

HANS (JOHANN) VON AACHEN
(Cologne 1552 - Prague 1615)

Portrait of Emperor Rudolf II
(1552-1612)

canvas, 60 x 48 cm, after 1595

Of all the painters Rudolf II called to his service in Prague,
Hans von Aachen was the one who had the closest relationship
with his imperial employer. He also bought works of art for
Rudolf and acted as a versatile counselor. The impressive
effect of this portrait is undoubtedly due to the painter's
intimate knowledge of the character of the introvert emperor.

FRANÇOIS CLOUET
(Tours ca.1510 - Paris 1572)

Portrait of Charles IX King of France
(1550-1574)

oak panel, 25 x 21 cm, ca. 1570

Clouet like Holbein was the son of a painter. The role he
played in Paris as court painter was similar to that of Holbein's
in London. He worked for Francis I from 1541 on. The Vienna
Gallery owns two portraits of Charles IX by François Clouet.
The one reproduced here shows the youthful king at the time of
his marriage to Archduchess Elizabeth of Austria in 1570. On
this occasion Archduke Ferdinand II of Tyrol, founder of the
Ambras collection, was proxy for the king at the wedding and
received this painting in sign of thanks.

LUCAS CRANACH THE ELDER
(Kronach 1472 - Weimar 1553)

Staghunt of Elector Frederick the Wise

poplar panel, 80 x 114 cm
1529

We have already encountered Lucas Cranach as the founder of
the Danubian School of painting (see p. 14). First active in
Vienna, he soon became the court painter for the prince elector
of Saxony in Wittenberg. The royal stag hunt which is
reproduced here is dated 1529 on the tree in the center. The
hunt could not however have taken place at this date for neither
Elector Frederick the Wise (1486-1525) nor Emperor
Maximilian I (1493-1519) were alive at the time. It is thus
clearly a commemorative painting, which was commissioned
by Elector John the Steadfast, who can be seen on the far right,
in memory of an earlier hunt.

LUCAS CRANACH THE YOUNGER ▶
(Wittenberg 1515 - Weimar 1586)

Portrait of a Woman

linden panel, 83 x 64 cm
1564

The son of the Wittenberg court painter of the same name, he
succeeded his father in the workshop. His portraits represent
the world of the German Protestant princes in the middle of the
16th century. Far from the large art centers, the ambient was
characterized by a rigid provincialism. This portrait of a
woman of 1564, as well as the companion portrait of a man,
was acquired by Archduke Leopold William. Kahnweiler sent
his friend Picasso a postcard of this portrait from Vienna, and
the painter based a famous linoleum print on it.

LUCAS VAN VALCKENBORCH

(Louvaine 1530 - Frankfurt 1597)

Winter Landscape
and
Spring Landscape

both on canvas, 117 x 198 cm
both 1586

Valckenborch began to work in 1570 for Archduke Matthia (later elected emperor), first in Antwerp, then in Linz and in Frankfurt. These two paintings were originally part of a series of seasons or months and show us, respectively, a Flemish village in a snow storm and a group of nobles on an outing in a grove, behind which Brussels can be seen. The city however is set into an imaginary landscape which does not correspond to geographical reality.

PIETER AERTSEN

(Amsterdam 1508 - 1575)

Still Life

oak panel, 60 x 101.5 cm
1552

Peasant Celebration

oak panel, cm 85 x 171
1550

While Aertsen's paintings were realistic depictions of men and objects, there was an underlying allegoric meaning which goes beyond daily reality and exhorts the observer to conversion and reflection in the Christian spirit. The famous scene in the house of Lazarus, taken from the Gospels, with Jesus telling the overly solicitous Martha that Mary, by listening to his word, has made the best choice, appears in the background of the still life.

PIETER BRUEGEL THE ELDER
(Breda? ca. 1525 - Brussels 1569)

Pieter Bruegel the Elder is now considered one of the greatest European painters. His masterworks were created in the brief period of about ten years (1559-1569) and for a long time they were not highly rated and were almost forgotten. Many of them survived because a few years after the death of the artist they were, in part, acquired by the Archduke Ernest, at the time governor of the Spanish Netherlands. After his death, they passed into the possession of Emperor Rudolf II who then also became an admirer and a fervid collector of Bruegel's works. Archduke Leopold William also contributed to the Hapsburg gallery's great collection of works by Bruegel; he acquired, among others, the painting of *Children's Games*. Some of the painter's most meaningful works include the imposing landscapes which originally constituted a cycle of the seasons consisting of six paintings, and the two compositions with peasants. Bruegel the artist was interested in man for his own sake, not necessarily imbuing his paintings with a historical or moralistic substratum. He does not ridicule the peasant, nor does he assume the role of accuser of the Spanish oppression. He is simply a profound thoughtful observer of life.

Children's Games

oak panel, 118 x 161 cm
1560

This painting, depicting over seventy children's games, is more than a simple compendium of popular Flemish life, but is also an allegorical depiction of the futility and inadequacy of all human toil.

PIETER BRUEGEL THE ELDER ▶
(Breda ? ca. 1525 - Brussels 1569)

Peasant Wedding
and
Peasant Dance

both oak panels, 114 x 164 cm
both ca. 1568

It was pictures like these which gave Pieter Bruegel the Elder his nickname of "Peasant Bruegel". He was, however, undoubtedly a townsman, and the story goes that he liked to go out into the country and observe the peasants in their revelries. The wedding picture shows us the banquet table in a barn, with the drinking and feasting guests, while at the lower end two peasants bring in the food which is handed to the guests by a third and equally robust figure. This group provides the composition with solidity but also with a twisting into the depth of the picture, of importance in the overall impression of space. Since the subjects of these two paintings are so closely related, they may have been companion pieces, although we have no way of knowing whether that was what the painter intended.
In any case, the *Peasant Dance* also depicts a rustic celebration, perhaps a fête.

PETER BRUEGEL THE ELDER

(Breda? ca. 1525 - Brussels 1569)

The Return of the Hunters (Winter)

oak panel, 117 x 162 cm

The Stormy Day (Just before Spring)

oak panel, 118 x 163 cm

Return of the Herd (Autumn)

oak panel, 117 x 159 cm

All three paintings are dated 1565

Bruegel illustrated the passing of time in the course of the year, not by depicting the twelve months or the four seasons as was normally the case, but in six paintings, each of which covers two months: thus the imposing painting of the hunters in the snow corresponds, probably, to the months of December and January, the somber expectation of spring, to February and March, and the herd returning home, to October and November. The panel with spring has been lost and the two summer panels, *Haymaking* and *Corn Harvest*, both once in the imperial gallery of Vienna, are now in Prague and in New York. The winter scene is the most famous of the series, in which Bruegel did much more than what was generally done in the typical extant depictions of the months for calendars or book illustrations. He presents us with a picture of all of creation in its changing seasonal appearances.

JAN BRUEGHEL THE ELDER

(Brussels 1568 - Antwerp 1625)

Large Bouquet of Flowers in a Wooden Tub

oak panel, 66 x 50.5 cm
1595

Jan Brueghel was the son of "Peasant Bruegel" but as an artist he depended little on his father and was more strongly influenced by his grandmother, the miniature painter Maria Bessemers. His nickname, "Velvet Brueghel", was probably due to the refined nature of his painting, although he was also known as "Flower Brueghel" because of his famous flower pieces. The panel illustrated here is the largest of Jan Brueghel's three Vienna flower pieces, which were added to the gallery by Archduke Leopold William. Brueghel's bouquets are not painted from real bunches of flowers but are artful compositions, severely symmetrical condensations. A scientific interest is combined with an esthetic effect and the symbolic meaning of many flowers. Everyone knows how important the tulip was in 17th century Holland, economically as well as otherwise.

PETER PAUL RUBENS
(Siegen 1577 - Antwerp 1640)

Rubens is the most forceful artistic personality in Northern
Europe, comparable only to the greatest Italian artists, such as
Raphael and Titian. With good reason, great stress is also laid
on the fact that, besides being a great man and an excellent
teacher, he was also a splendid organizer of his important
workshop. A long sojourn in Italy in his youth, two trips to
Spain, four to Paris and one to England, in which he was also
entrusted with political-diplomatic missions by the Hapsburg
governor, gave him a chance to come into contact with
everything that was going on in the art world of his time, as
well as with the masterpieces of the past. Rubens married
twice, and the ideal woman found throughout his work can be
identified with Isabella Brant, his first wife, as well as in the
features of his second wife, Helena Fourment.

The Four Continents

canvas, 209 x 284 cm
ca. 1615

At the beginning of the 17th century, Australia had not yet
been discovered. The allegory of the world is therefore
depicted by four female figures and the personifications of the
great rivers. On the left, Europe is flanked by the river god
Danube (with the oar), Africa is shown as a Mauretanian
woman with the Nile and a crocodile, while the figures on the
right side represent America with the Amazon River and Asia
with the Ganges. At their feet, a tiger defends its cubs.

PETER PAUL RUBENS ▶
(Siegen 1577 - Antwerp 1640)

The Madonna Appears to St. Ildefonsus

oak panel, 352 x 236 cm
ca. 1632
(central part of the Ildefonsus altarpiece)

The Ildefonsus altarpiece is the main work of Rubens' latter
years and was painted entirely by the artist. The altarpiece is
dedicated to a holy archbishop of Toledo to whom Archduke
Albrecht, governor of the Netherlands, was particularly devoted
and was offered in his memory by his widow, the Infanta
Isabella Clara Eugenia. Both the Hapsburg princes are shown
on the wings of the altar, together with their patron saints, St.
Albertus Magnus and St. Elizabeth of Thuringia. When the
altarpiece was closed, the picture on the shutters was of the
Holy Family under an apple tree, now removed. In the central
portion of the triptych, illustrated here, Rubens shows St.
Ildefonsus kneeling before the Virgin who, surrounded by
female saints, hands him a chasuble. The visionary quality of
the theme, the apparition of the Mother of God in the church, is
made credible by the brilliant painterly execution and the
glowing force of the colors. The altarpiece comes from St-
Jacques-sur-Coudenberg in Brussels. When the Jesuit order
was suppressed, Maria Theresa acquired this, as well as the
other large Rubens altarpieces, for the Vienna Gallery.

PETER PAUL RUBENS
(Siegen 1577 - Antwerp 1640)

Helena Fourment, the Painter's Second Wife ("The Little Fur")

oak panel, 176 x 83 cm
ca. 1635/40

Rubens apparently painted this portrait of his second wife for himself and he also called it by the name that has come down to us. Admired even at the time for its immediateness, the natural pose of the figure and the marvelous painting, this work dates to the artist's last years.The Vienna gallery also owns his last self-portrait from these same years.

PETER PAUL RUBENS
(Siegen 1577 - Antwerp 1640)

The Hermit and Sleeping Angelica

oak panel, 43 x 66 cm
before 1630

The theme of the picture is a scene from Ariosto's "Orlando Furioso", while Rubens found his pictorial model in a famous painting by Titian, *The Andrii*. This intimate work betrays the strong influence that Venetian painting exerted on Rubens.

PETER PAUL RUBENS
(Siegen 1577 - Antwerp 1640)

Self-portrait

canvas, 109.5 x 85 cm
ca.1638/40

In this last self-portrait, Rubens appears
not only as a great artist but also as a
successful ambassador and a
distinguished cavalier. It was not until
the first third of the 18th century, in the
time of Emperor Charles VI, that this
self-portrait and *The Little Fur* became
part of the imperial collections.

PETER PAUL RUBENS
(Siegen 1577 - Antwerp 1640)

Head of Medusa

canvas, 68.5 x 118 cm
ca. 1617/18

The virtuoso depiction of this
frightening theme has always greatly
impressed spectators. The painting is an
important example of collaboration
between the master and his pupils, for
while the terrible head of the Gorgon
Medusa was painted by Rubens himself,
the animals are by Frans Snyder and
Paul de Vos.

35

◄ ANTON VAN DYCK
(Antwerp 1599 - London 1641)

**Madonna and the Child, St. Rosalie and
Sts. Peter and Paul**

canvas, 275 x 210 cm
1629

This great altarpiece was painted by Van Dyck for the
Confraternity of Recollects in Antwerp, to which he
belonged. The Confraternity depended on the Jesuit order
and when this was broken up, the painting and the one
across from it were acquired by the Gallery, on behalf of
Emperor Joseph, in 1776.

ANTON VAN DYCK
(Antwerp 1599 - London 1641)

**The Mystical Betrothal of the Blessed Herman Joseph
with the Madonna**

canvas, 160 x 128 cm
1630

Van Dyck, Rubens' greatest pupil, represented a vision
in this altar painting just as his master had done in the
Ildefonsus altarpiece. Van Dyck's subject is the
apparition of the Madonna to the Praemonstratensian
monk Herman Joseph. A mystical betrothal with the
Mother of God is indicated by the touching of fingertips.
This painting is typical of Counter-Reformation religious
sentiment.

ANTON VAN DYCK
(Antwerp 1599 - London 1641)

Prince Rupert (with the Great Dane) and Charles Louis of the Palatinate

both on canvas, 175 x 96 cm
both 1631/32

Van Dyck here portrayed two brothers who shared a common fate: both were expelled from their country since they were sons of the so-called Winterkönig (Winter king) of Bohemia, Frederick of the Palatinate. They grew up at the court of London. Prince Rupert became a general and admiral in the service of England; he was greatly interested in art and was known as the Mad Cavalier. Prince Charles Louis struggled for years to regain possession of his right to succession and when, with the Peace of Westphalia, in 1648, his title of Elector Palatinate was restored, he returned to Heidelberg.

JACOB JORDAENS
(Antwerp 1593 - 1678)

▶

The Bean King's Festival

canvas, 242 x 300 cm
ca. 1655

In many European countries a cake or a pastry with a bean baked into it is eaten on the feast of Epiphany. The person to whose lot it falls is king for the day, choosing a queen and a court.

JAN STEEN
(Leyden 1626 - 1679)

The World Upside Down

canvas, 105 x 145 cm
1663

In a highly entertaining manner, the
painter and host of Leyden shows us
what happens when we let ourselves be
governed by the intemperance and by
lack of restraint.

DAVID TENIERS THE YOUNGER
(Antwerp 1610 - Brussels 1690)

Archduke Leopold William in his Gallery in Brussels

canvas, 123 x 163 cm
ca.1651

Archduke Leopold William, who has already been named in the introduction to this book as the real founder of the Picture Gallery (Gemäldegalerie), often commissioned his court painter David Teniers to paint the artfully arranged interiors of his Brussels collection. He then used these paintings as gifts. They are of particular interest for the history of the Picture Gallery.

SAMUEL VAN HOOGSTRAETEN
(Dordrecht 1626 - 1678)

Man at the Window

canvas, 111 x 86.5 cm
1653

This curious "trompe l'oeil" painting is thought to be the portrait of the rabbi Jom-Tob Lipmann Heller (1579-1654), active first in Vienna and then in Prague. The portrait dates to the artist's Viennese period when he was employed as painter at the court of the emperor, Ferdinand III.

JAN VERMEER VAN DELFT

(Delft 1632 - 1675)

Allegory of Painting

canvas, 120 x 100 cm
ca. 1670

This important work by the painter is one of the greatest masterpieces of Dutch painting and is often called "The Painter in his Studio". But apparently Vermeer's intentions were to paint an allegory of painting. He therefore also probably identified himself with the painter in the picture, who ensures his fame for posterity by his work. That is why the female model with her book, trumpet and laurel wreath is represented as an allegory of Fame.

GERARD TER BORCH
(Zwolle 1617 - Deventer 1681)

The Apple Peeler

canvas on wood, 36.3 x 30.7 cm
ca. 1661

In Dutch 17th-century painting a heretofore unheard of specialization developed. There were specialists in still life, flower pieces, landscapes, portraits, religious and historical events, and also some who specialized in interiors. Ter Borch often painted intimate representations of one or more figures in a room. In this picture, too, the tender but trusting relationship between mother and child is perfectly depicted.

JACOB VAN RUISDAEL
(Haarlem 1628 - Amsterdam 1682)

The Forest

canvas, 139 x 180 cm
ca. 1660

Jacob van Ruisdael is the most important representative of Dutch landscape painting and his main work, *The Forest*, is a painting whose praises Goethe sang because of its particular beauty. As was the case with the Dutch flower pieces and still lifes, this landscape painting is not a simple copy of nature, but every detail has been thought over and the whole thing arranged and composed.

SIMON DE VLIEGER

(Rotterdam 1602 - Weesp 1653)

Visit to the Fleet

oak panel, 71 x 92 cm
1649

This is one of the first pictures of a theme the "Dutch" nation of navigators was particularly fond of. The event described is probably the inspection of the Dutch fleet before an expedition into Flanders by the prince of Orange, Frederick Henry II, in 1646.

PIETER DE HOOCH

(Rotterdam 1629 - Amsterdam after 1684)

Mother and Child next to the Crib and with a Servant-maid

canvas, 64 x 76 cm
ca. 1663/65

Pieter de Hooch contrasts Ter Borch's quiet interior with the industrious mother as the focal point of the home. The picture irradiates the proverbial cleanliness, well-being and self-complacency of Calvinist Holland.

REMBRANDT HARMENSZ VAN RIJN

(Leiden 1606 - Amsterdam 1669)

Large Self-portrait

canvas 112 x 81.5 cm
1652

Small Self-portrait

walnut panel, 48.8 x 40.6 cm
ca. 1657

Titus van Rijn, the Artist's Son, Reading

canvas, 70.5 x 64 cm
ca. 1656/57

Rembrandt was more than just the most important of Dutch painters. While he was not a specialist in any particular theme, as were most of his colleagues, he was a painter who mastered almost all subjects and was particularly interested in biblical and historical events. The Vienna Gallery owns no such painting, but it does have altogether seven portraits by Rembrandt, including three self-portraits, the portrait of his mother as the

prophetess Hannah, and of his son Titus as a reading youth. The three portraits shown here are from the middle of the 17th century, the period in which a change in the taste of the public considerably diminished his commissions. He gradually became poorer, withdrew, an embittered man, and in 1656 had to sell all he owned - his art collection and his large house. His children, including his son Titus, his fourth child from his marriage to Saskia, died when he was still alive.

The self-portraits of these years express a profound grief. Rembrandt, as no other master, had the ability to completely comprehend other people was well as himself and to reproduce them in paintings. Forgoing almost all details, he concentrated on the representation of the face, which glows out of the darkness of the painting. A puzzled wondering human being, whose greatest achievement lies in the inexorable knowledge of himself, confronts us in the small self-portrait of Vienna from the year 1657.

In these later years in which the *Titus* was also painted, Rembrandt's style of painting is broad, with the colors limited to a few tones between brown and gray, from which the light spots of color glow forth, and the essential parts, such as the face, the hands and the book of the youth, stand out.

ANDREA MANTEGNA
(Isola di Carturo 1431 - Mantua 1506)

St. Sebastian

poplar panel, 68 x 30 cm
ca. 1460

The new problem faced by Italian 15th century art, which had its centers in Padua as well as Florence and Venice, clearly comes to the fore in the figure of St. Sebastian. Mantegna strove to represent the body correctly, to comprehend the space from a scientific point of view. This is clear from the way in which Mantegna represents the body of the martyr as a sculpture, in other words, stressing the three-dimensionality. The figure of Sebastian seems to be made of stone, part of the architectural ruins behind him. The figure of a knight can also be distinguished in the clouds above him, a reference to the Theodoric relief on the facade of S. Zeno in Verona.

PISANELLO
(Pisa ca. 1395 - 1455)

Portrait of the Emperor Sigismund
(1369-1437)

parchment on panel, 64 x 49 cm
1433

Sigismund, king of Hungary and Bohemia, was the last emperor of the Holy Roman Empire to belong to the house of Luxembourg. Pisanello can be included in the list of the most influential and sensitive artists of all times. He is the most important Italian master in the period of transition from the Middle Ages to modern times.

ANTONELLO DA MESSINA
(Messina ca. 1430 - 1479)

Madonna with Saints Nicholas and Anastasias (left),
Domenico and Orsola (S. Cassiano Altarpiece)

panel, 115 (56) x 134 cm
1476

What we have here is only a fragment of the original work. The
painting is composed of three parts which, up to about 1620,
constituted with other panels, now lost, the great altarpiece of
S. Cassiano in Venice. The Sicilian Antonello sojourned in
Venice in 1475/75, where his pictorial technique, a mixture of
French and Flemish currents introduced to Naples and Sicily by
the Aragonese rulers, was enthusiastically received. Such
luminous and brilliant colors had never before been seen in the
painting of Northern Italy.

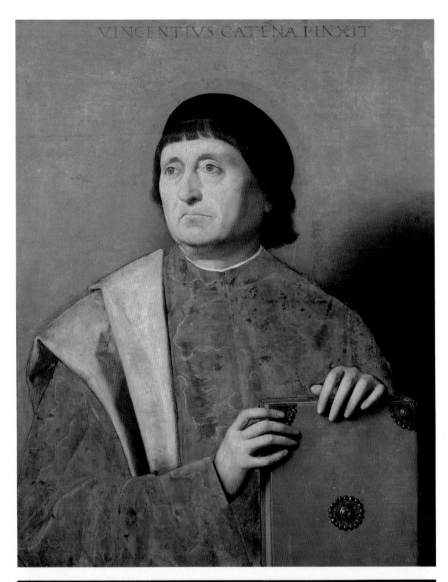

VINCENZO CATENA
(ca. 1480 - Venice 1531)

Portrait of a Man with a Book

panel, 79 x 59.5 cm
ca. 1520

Catena, a pupil, like Giorgione and Titian, of Giovanni Bellini, remained basically under the influence of this great Venetian master, even though this painting dates to the year after the master's death. In addition to a precise perspective rendering of space, the painter tries to recreate the light that plays around the body and modifies the color intensities.

GIOVANNI BELLINI
(Venice 1432 - 1516)

Young Woman at Her Toilette

poplar panel, 62 x 79 cm
1515

Giovanni Bellini was one of the principal Venetian masters in the second half of the 15th century, and was also influenced by Mantegna, as can be seen in his *Presentation in the Temple* in the Vienna Gallery. On the other hand, in his old age in 1515 he was influenced by the art of the younger generation, to which at the time Giorgione and Titian belonged. The similarity of the composition of the picture shown here with Titian's *Gypsy Madonna* (page 50) is obvious.

GIORGIONE
(Giorgio da Castelfranco) ▶
(Castelfranco Veneto 1477 - Venice 1510)

The Three Philosophers

canvas, 123.8 x 144.5 cm
ca. 1508

Giorgione, a pupil of Bellini's, who also influenced his teacher with his new art, as was noted in the preceding caption, painted only a few pictures in his short life. Not long after his death, their thematic meaning was no longer clear. The *Three Philosophers* is one of these enigmatic works. The celestial map which the oldest of them unrolls and the astronomical instruments the youngest man holds have also led to their being called "astronomers" or "mathematicians".

In consideration of the allegorical significance of
some of the details in the painting, it has been
suggested that the three men are the three Magi, who
are making calculations on the appearance of the star
which is to announce the birth of Christ. Apart from
its complicated content, the painting conveys a
poetical, lyrical atmosphere which distinguishes
Giorgione's other works in the Vienna Gallery, even
if not to the same extent.

GIORGIONE
(Giorgio da Castelfranco)
(Castelfranco Veneto 1477 - Venice 1510)

Boy with an Arrow

poplar panel, 48 x 42 cm
ca. 1505

Giorgione almost seems to have succeeded in
painting the air that fills the space. The boy looks as
if he were enveloped in a subtle mist which softens
and blurs the outlines and blends the colors.

TITIAN (Tiziano Vecellio)
(Pieve di Cadore ca. 1488 - Venice 1576)

Gypsy Madonna

panel, 65.8 x 83.5 cm
ca. 1510

Titian's early works are hard to catalog in time and this depends partly on the fact that the date of his birth is uncertain. The *Gypsy Madonna*, which may have been painted around 1510, is very similar to Giorgione's works. But the importance of color for Titian is already apparent here.

TITIAN (Tiziano Vecellio)
(Pieve di Cadore ca. 1488 - Venice 1576)

Ecce Homo

canvas, 242 x 361 cm
1543

A survey of Titian's collected works, which are distributed in
many galleries throughout the world, is difficult indeed. Both
former Hapsburg collections in Vienna and Madrid own some
of the most important and finest works of the master who
during his lifetime was already famous as Emperor Charles V's
court painter and who was highly esteemed as the greatest of
all painters by the reigning Hapsburg family. The large altar
painting *Ecce Homo*, dated 1543, shows Titian under the
influence of the Mannerists. This is revealed in the complicated
structure of the composition, in the crowd of people at the foot
of the stairs, and in the twisted figure of the shield-bearer in the
foreground. Titian has left us a series of portraits in this
painting. Pontius Pilate, showing Christ to the crowd, bears the
features of the poet Pietro Aretino, the two riders to the right
are Sultan Suleiman and a general of Charles V, or Charles V
himself. The Doge and Titian's daughter, Lavinia, can also be
recognized.

TITIAN (Tiziano Vecellio)
(Pieve di Cadore ca. 1488 - Venice 1576)

Danae

canvas, 135 x 152 cm
after 1554

The myth of Danae and Jupiter, who visited Danae in the form
of a rain of gold, was painted by Titian both for the Hapsburg
court in Madrid, that is for King Philip II, and for his cousin,
Emperor Maximilian II, in Vienna. The second painting was
bought, around 1600, by Emperor Rudolph II for his gallery.

TITIAN (Tiziano Vecellio)
(Pieve di Cadore ca. 1488 - Venice 1576)

Girl with a Fur

canvas, 95 x 63 cm
ca. 1535

In a perfectly natural way, Titian has set two contrasting
movements one next to the other - vertical and horizontal lines,
light and shade. The result is a portrait of absolute tranquility,
with perfect spatial and corporeal illusion.

TITIAN (Tiziano Vecellio)
(Pieve di Cadore ca. 1488 - Venice 1576)

Isabella d'Este
(1474-1539)

canvas, 102 x 64 cm
ca. 1534/36

Isabella, daughter of Ercole I, duke of Modena and Ferrara, and
of Eleonora of Aragon, married Marchese Francesco Gonzaga
of Mantua in 1490. A great patron of the arts, in 1511 she
had her portrait painted by Francesco Francia. This portrait,
which no longer exists, was "copied" by Titian a quarter
of a century later.

TITIAN (Tiziano Vecellio)   ▶
(Pieve di Cadore ca. 1488 - Venice 1576)

Portrait of Jacopo da Strada

canvas, 125 x 95 cm
ca. 1567/68

The multifaceted personality of this proud gentleman whom Titian immortalized in one of his late portraits made him a typical High Renaissance man. As a connoisseur of art and an architect, Jacopo da Strada served in various courts, in Vienna from 1557 on and in the Prague of the Hapsburg emperors from 1577 on. He became indispensable to them as expert and agent. As such he came into contact with Titian, who in this portrait gives us the restlessness and egoism of the dealer, intent on acquiring the best pieces for his lord but basically interested only in what was to his own advantage.

LORENZO LOTTO
(Venice 1480 - Loreto 1556)

Portrait of a Youth in Front of a White Curtain

linden panel, 42.3 x 53.3 cm
ca. 1508

Although Lorenzo Lotto came from Venice and painted his early works, such as this portrait of a youth in front of a white curtain, in the laguna city, he later worked in many other Italian cities. The portrait shown here, which can be numbered as one of his most beautiful, is effective thanks to the immediacy with which the young man stands before us. What fascinates us most in this picture is not Titian's rich range of colors or Giorgione's poetical atmosphere, but the lifelikeness and strength that characterize Dürer's portraits.

LORENZO LOTTO
(Venice 1480 - Loreto 1556)

Madonna and Child with Sts. Catherine and James

canvas, 113.5 x 152 cm
ca. 1530

The painter's restless compositions, in which one seems to be aware of the relationships between the various figures, reveal the same intense sensitivity that comes to the fore in his portraits.

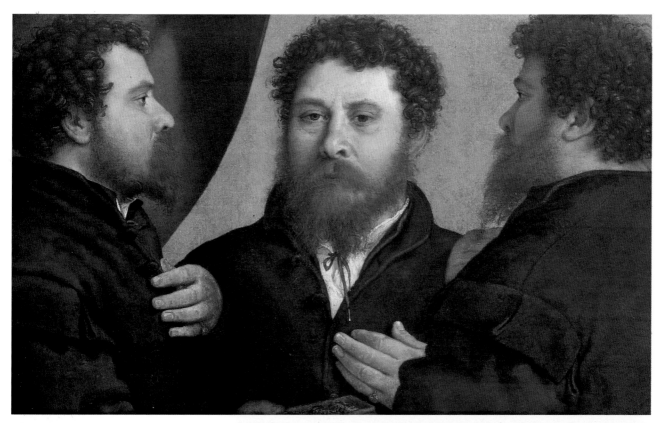

LORENZO LOTTO
(Venice 1480 - Loreto 1556)

Triple Portrait of a Man

canvas, 52 x 79 cm
ca. 1525/35

This original and enigmatic portrait of a
man with a red beard may be that of the
goldsmith Bartolomeo Carpan of
Treviso. With its illusion of a three-
dimensional reality, this artefice, if
nothing more, offers the person depicted
a new form of self perception.

BERNARDINO LICINIO
(ca. 1485 - Venice 1550)

Portrait of Ottavio Grimani,
Procurator of S. Marco

canvas, 114 x 95 cm
1541

Like the other Venetian painters, Licinio
was also profoundly influenced by
Giorgione's poetic naturalism. The
personage shown was a powerful
Venetian dignitary for, as procurator, he
could dispose of the State treasure of the
Doge's Republic, which was kept in St.
Mark's.

PERUGINO
(Perugia ca. 1445/48 - Fontignano, near Città della Pieve 1523)

Baptism of Christ

panel, 30 x 23.3 cm
ca. 1498/1500

Perugino was wont to concentrate on the essential part of the theme, so that sometimes his compositions seem overly simple, almost cold, compared with the pictorial richness of the Venetians. An example is the fine landscape, somehow almost lifeless, in the background of the Baptism of Christ. Starting from Perugino, Raphael developed his art to the highest perfection.

FRA BARTOLOMEO
(Florence 1475 - 1517)

Presentation of Christ in the Temple

poplar panel, 155 x 159 cm
1516

Fra Bartolomeo painted this altarpiece for the Novitiate Chapel in the Dominican convent of S. Marco in Florence, where he had entered as a monk in 1501.

RAPHAEL (Raffaello Sanzio)
(Urbino 1483 - Rome 1520)

St. Margaret

poplar panel, 192 x 122 cm

Various pictures of St. Margaret as dragon slayer by Raphael are known, although doubt has been thrown on whether they are by Raphael's own hand. In the Vienna panel, Raphael's pupils also probably either executed the painting or collaborated. In this connection the name of Giulio Romano is often made. Archduke Leopold William though still listed the painting as an original by Raphael in his inventory.

RAPHAEL (Raffaello Sanzio)
(Urbino 1483 - Rome 1520)

Madonna del Prato

poplar panel, 113 x 88.5 cm
1505 or 1506

The importance of Raphael for European history of art and thought is well known. There is something magic about his paintings, especially his representations of the Madonna, that is difficult to describe. Since he painted so many, they acquired nicknames through the years. The Vienna Madonna was formerly known as the "Belvedere Madonna" after the old gallery building. The name by which she is now commonly known refers to the open landscape in which the full figure of the Madonna appears. Originally the idea for this type of figure came from Leonardo da Vinci. The *Madonna del Prato* was sold from the Florentine palazzo of the Taddei family in 1662 to an Austrian archduke and has been in Vienna since 1773.

PARMIGIANINO (Francesco Mazzola)
(Parma 1503 - Casalmaggiore 1540)

Self-portrait in a Convex Mirror

circular poplar panel, diam. 24 cm
1523

One of the most unusual paintings is the self-portrait which Parmigianino painted on a convex wooden panel in his attempt to reproduce precisely the distortion of a convex mirror. Art history sees this painting of 1523 as the "incunabula" of Mannerism, an artistic period between the Renaissance and the Baroque, which questioned the laws of perspective and other artistic achievements and sought to gain the attention of the public through its extravagant compositions, an example of which is the striking "Fall of Paul" (see facing page).

GIUSEPPE ARCIMBOLDO
(Milan 1527 - 1593)

Summer - Water

lindenwood panels, respectively 67 x 50.8 cm and
66.5 x 50.5 cm, respectively 1563 and 1566

The Kunsthistorisches Museum still owns four paintings, part of a series of the four elements and the four seasons, painted by Arcimboldo between 1563 and 1566 for Emperor Maximilian II in Vienna, where he worked many years as court painter. When Emperor Rudolf II later transferred his court to Prague, Arcimboldo returned to Milan.

PARMIGIANINO (Francesco Mazzola)

(Parma 1503 - Casalmaggiore 1540)

Conversion of St. Paul

canvas, 177.5 x 128.5 cm
1527/28

That decisive moment in the history of the world, when Saul, the persecutor of Christians, falls from his horse, as if struck by lightning and blinded by divine light, then to rise as Paul and from that moment on preach Christ and His Resurrection, was often represented in works of art, but rarely in as dramatic and surprising a manner as here by Parmigianino. After a thorough restoration, this splendid Viennese painting with its irridescent colors reveals itself as one of the painter's masterpieces.

PARIS BORDONE
(Treviso 1500 - Venice 1571)

Allegory

canvas, 111,5 x 174.5 cm
ca. 1550

The picture is easy to describe. A couple of lovers, shown as
the god of war Mars, dressed in armor, and the goddess of love
Venus, are crowned with a myrtle wreath by a cupid. From the
point of view of art however, the effect is surprising. The
colors, broken up into spots, with their luminous reflections
and irridescent effects, create a disturbing, almost unnatural,
erotic atmosphere, particularly in keeping with the theme.

CORREGGIO (Antonio Allegri)

(Correggio, 1489 - Reggio Emilia 1534)

Jupiter and Io

canvas, 163 x 70 cm
ca. 1530

The Rape of Ganymede

canvas, 162 x 73 cm
ca. 1530

These two mythological scenes belonged to a series of four paintings, whose subject was Jupiter's amorous escapades. The other two paintings, a "Leda" and a "Danae", are now in Rome and in Berlin. The entire series belonged to the Hapsburgs, first in Madrid, later in Prague. In both of the Vienna paintings Correggio represents the key event of the myth, specifically the embrace of the nymph Io by Jupiter in the form of a cloud, and the moment in which Jupiter's eagle abducts the shepherd boy, Ganymede, into Olympus, where he is to live as cup-bearer of the gods.

◄ VERONESE (Paolo Caliari)
(Verona 1528 - Venice 1588)

Lucrezia

canvas, 109 x 90.5 cm
after 1580

Venus and Adonis

canvas, 68 x 52 cm
late work (ca. 1586)

Veronese's fame was due first of all to his capacity to articulate the composition of his picture harmoniously, which was then transformed into a trenchant event by his masterly use of color chords. This skill of Veronese's, apparently "purely" decorative, is actually also dramatic art, as shown by the painting of the suicide of Lucrezia, and a sensually erotic narrative art. Of the great Venetian masters, Veronese is the one who most crucially influenced the development of 18th century art when the beauty of Venetian painting blossomed forth, once more, in all its splendor.

TINTORETTO (Jacopo Robusti)
(Venice 1518 - 1594)

The Queen of Sheba before Solomon

Belshazzar's Feast

David Carrying the Holy Ark

The Promise to David that his Issue would be Eternal

four cassoni
spruce, ca 30 x 156 cm
ca. 1543/44

Susanna and the Elders

canvas, 146 x 193.5 cm
ca. 1560

Titian's pictorial qualities left their mark on all of 16th century Venetian painting, including Tintoretto and Veronese. From Tintoretto's numerous works, five episodes from the Old Testament are illustrated here. The four *cassoni* present a genre of decorative painting on furniture or wall panels. *Susanna and the Elders* is the great masterpiece of the young Titian, a lively bold composition, full of contrasts: youth and age, light and shade, purity and vice. Susanna, like the Roman Lucrezia, is the symbol of candor and sincerity.

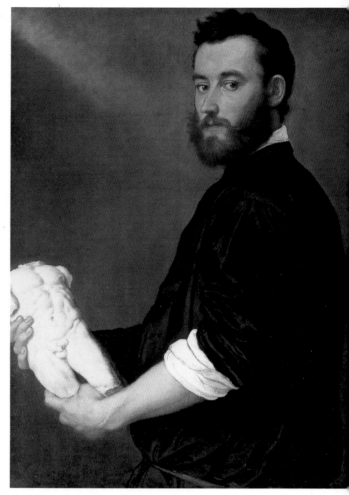

NICOLÒ DELL'ABBATE
(Modena ca. 1510 - Fontainebleau 1571?)

Portrait of a Man with a Parrot

canvas, 125 x 109 cm
ca. 1552/55

Abbate, one of the great masters of Mannerism, weds the tranquil, ideal corporeity of Raphael with the lively sense of color of the Venetians. The result is a highly incisive portrait.

GIOVANNI BATTISTA MORONI
(Albino, near Bergamo ca. 1520 - Bergamo 1578)

The Sculptor Alessandro Vittoria
(1525-1608)

canvas, 87.5 x 70 cm
ca. 1552/53

Moroni is known primarily as a portrait painter, and was highly successful among his contemporaries. In the portrait of the famous Venetian sculptor, reproduced here, the sober and realistic attitude of the subject is coupled with a soft atmospheric tonality. The head, suddenly turning to look at the viewer, and the decisive gesture with which he displays the antique torso, let us feel the physical closeness as well as the spiritual presence of the artist.

JACOPO BASSANO (da Ponte)   ▶
(Bassano ca. 1515 - 1592)

Adoration of the Three Kings

canvas, 92 x 117.5 cm
ca. 1560/65

Jacopo da Ponte, a contemporary of Tintoretto's, descended from one of the branches of a family of painters in the Venetian province, from the "mainland" in other words. *The Adoration of the Christ Child by the Three Magi* is one of his finest and most mature works. The artist's predilection for life in the country and a self-assured naturalness are also evident in this painting.

ORAZIO GENTILESCHI (Lomi)
(Pisa 1563 - London 1639)

Rest on the Flight to Egypt

canvas, 138.5 x 216 cm
1625/28

Gentileschi can be counted as one of the painters influenced by Caravaggio's naturalistic experience (see the following pages). His atmospheric painting shows us Joseph, tired out and sleeping on his bundle, while Mary with maternal serenity and naturalness nurses the Child. The treatment of light and shade in this tranquil scene also derives from Caravaggio.

GUERCINO
(Giovanni Francesco Barbieri)
(Cento 1591 - Bologna 1666)

The Return of the Prodigal Son

canvas, 107 x 143.5 cm
1619

The disturbing chiaroscuro in which the
half figures in this biblical scene are
immersed helps us understand the drama
of the event. The son, who had been
thought lost, returns home after having
squandered his part of his inheritance
and is lovingly welcomed back.

CARAVAGGIO
(Michelangelo Merisi)
(Caravaggio 1571 - Porto Ercole 1610)

 **David with the Head of Goliath**

panel, 90.5 x 116 cm
ca. 1606

Madonna of the Rosary

canvas, 364 x 249 cm.
1606/07

The way in which Michelangelo Merisi,
who orginally came from a place near
Milan, understood and represented
reality differed greatly from that of his
famous contemporaries, such as Guido
Reni. His inflexible quest for truth was
accompanied by an uncontrollable
temper. His David, who has already
killed the giant Goliath with his
slingshot and cut off his head, is the
young shepherd boy described in the
Bible, but is also what the painter saw
around Rome every day.
His large altar painting however
illustrates a legend which was often
represented at the end of the 15th
century in connection with the
promotion of rosary prayers. The legend
narrates that St. Dominic received a
rosary from the Madonna. In
Caravaggio's painting, the pressing
crowd sees only the saint and the rosary
in his hands, while he himself has the
vision of the Madonna. The Dominican
Order considered itself called upon to
fight the heathens and heretics. At the
end of the 16th century , it was the
Turks against whom they were called to
battle. The victory over the Turkish
fleet in the battle of Lepanto was
attributed to the intervention of the
Madonna and countless churches were
dedicated to her as the "Madonna of the
Rosary". Caravaggio's naturalism was
disdained by many of his
contemporaries. In 1620 his *Madonna
of the Rosary* was in the Dominican
church in Antwerp and was bought for
the imperial gallery in 1781.

GUIDO RENI
(Bologna 1575 - 1642)

The Baptism of Christ

canvas, 263.5 x 186.5 cm.
ca. 1620

Towards the end of the 16th century a group of Italian painters, most important of whom were Annibale Carracci and Guido Reni, developed an idealistic art that was modelled on the antique and on Raphael's painting. Reni's most impressive altar painting clearly demonstrates the ideals of these artists. The composition is clear, the movements and gestures of the figures noble. The task of art, to convincingly convey a theme of faith, has been successfully achieved.

ANNIBALE CARRACCI
(Bologna 1560 - Rome 1609)

Pietà

copper, 41 x 60 cm

The forcefulness of Annibale Carracci's small *Pietà* is in striking contrast to the impressive size of Guido Reni's altarpiece. The theme of grief and sorrow is just as convincingly represented with the same clarity of composition.

BERNARDO STROZZI

(Genoa 1581 - Venice 1644)

Lute-player

canvas, 92 x 76 cm
ca. 1631/35

The Prophet Eliah and the Widow of Sarepta

canvas, 106 x 138 cm
ca. 1640/44

The Vienna Gallery has a series of fine paintings by Strozzi,
who at the age of 17 entered the Capuchin order and was
therefore also called "Il Cappuccino". After an eventful life as
a secular priest and then as engineer in the port of Genoa, he
lived in Venice from 1631 to his death. His spirited
compositions, such as the *Lute-player*, were influenced by the
example of the great Flemish painter Rubens. By showing
the meeting of the prophet with the poor widow the artist
has depicted the miracle of giving and receiving, subtly
stressing the spiritual atmosphere by the crossing movement of
the hands.

NICOLAS POUSSIN
(Villiers 1594 - Rome 1665)

The Destruction of the Temple in Jerusalem by Titus

canvas, 148 x 199 cm
1638

One of the most important representatives of the artistic trend
set by Annibale Carracci was Nicolas Poussin from Normandy.
In 1624 he moved to Rome, where the ancient architecture and
the landscape of the Eternal City made a great impression on
him. Poussin painted the *Destruction of the Temple in
Jerusalem by Titus* for Cardinal Francesco Barberini, who gave
it to a legate as a gift for Emperor Ferdinand III.

GUIDO CAGNACCI
(Sant'Arcangelo di Romagna 1601 - Vienna 1663)

The Death of Cleopatra

canvas, 140 x 160 cm
1657/58

Emperor Leopold I called Cagnacci to the Vienna court in
1657. His works of this period are finely balanced
compositions with a feeling for color and an accentuated
realism, to be seen, for example, in the gestures of the servants
who excitedly gather around their queen, as she dies from the
bite of a poisonous snake rather than fall into the hands of the
Romans.

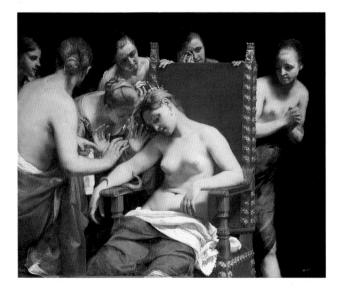

DOMENICO FETTI ▶
(Rome, ca. 1588/90 - Venice 1623)

Galathea and Polyphemus

Perseus Freeing Andromeda

Eros Mourning the Dead Leander

*all: poplar wood, respectively 41 x 97 cm, 40.5 x 72.5 cm,
41 x 97 cm ca. 1621/22*

These small paintings with subjects derived from Greek
mythology once probably decorated furniture, and show us the
high level of the artist's pictorial culture, best appreciated by a
connoisseur of painting.

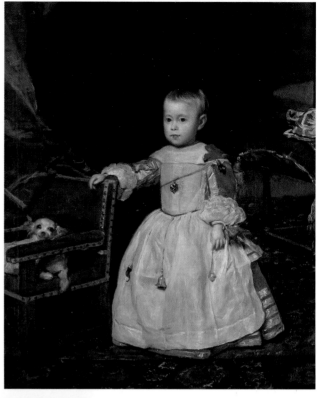

DIEGO RODRIGUEZ DE SILVA Y VELÁZQUEZ
(Seville 1599 - Madrid 1660)

The Infanta Margarita Teresa, Five Years Old, in a White Dress
(1651-1673)

canvas, 105 x 88 cm
ca. 1656

The Infanta Margarita Teresa in a Blue Dress
(1651-1673)

canvas 127 x 107 cm
1659

The Infante Felipe Prospero
(1657-1661)

canvas, 128.5 x 100 cm
1659

Not only is the 17th century the greatest century in Spanish painting, but it is also the greatest century in European portrait painting. Especially the Hapsburg princes, who reigned in Madrid, Brussels and Vienna, kept the best portrait painters of their times busy: Rubens, Van Dyck and Velázquez. The

Vienna paintings by Velázquez were all sent to Vienna as gifts by King Philip IV. Most of them were portraits of children whose purpose was not merely that of delighting the imperial cousin, but was also a question of family politics. The Infanta Margarita Teresa had been designated as a future empress, and throughout the years three portraits of her were sent to her bridgroom. The loveliest was the one of the eight-year old Infanta in a blue party dress. The portrait of her younger brother, Felipe Prospero, more than that of the Infanta, reveals Velázquez's ability to grasp the soul of a person, a gift his contemporary Rembrandt was also blessed with.

JUAN BAUTISTA MAZO
(Beteta, Cuenca ca. 1612 - Madrid 1667)

The Artist's Family

canvas, 148 x 174.5 cm
ca. 1664/65

Mazo's family pays a visit to the atelier of the grandfather, the painter of the royal court, Velázquez, standing near his easel in the background.
The four youths in dark clothing at the left are Mazo's sons from his first marriage with Francisca, Velázquez' daughter. His second wife sits on the right with her four children.

GIOVAMBATTISTA TIEPOLO

(Venice 1696 - Madrid 1770)

The Death of the Consul L. J. Brutus in a Duel with Aruns

canvas, 383 x 182 cm
1728/30

Tiepolo not only frescoed countless
Venetian palazzi and villas on the
mainland, but also painted series of large
canvases to be used in their decoration.
The Vienna Gallery possesses two such
paintings from the decorative ensemble
of the large salon of the Ca' Dolfin,
which consisted of ten pictures of
varying sizes. The rest are divided
between Saint Petersburg and New
York. The so-called cavalry combat
shown here represents a Roman and
Etruscan battle scene, as handed down
by Livy. At the time, the first Consul of
Rome, L. J. Brutus, was killed in a duel
with Aruns, the son of Tarquinius
Superbus, the last of the legendary kings
of Rome. Aruns too was mortally
wounded in the duel. The second
painting in the series, also in Vienna,
represents the great Punic general
Hannibal contemplating the severed
head of his brother.

FRANCESCO GUARDI
(Venice 1712 - 1793)

Pilgrims on a Broken Bridge

canvas, 122 x 172 cm
1763

The Dominican saint Gonzalo di
Amarante comes to succor pilgrims in
danger of death. The painting is
executed in a virtuoso style, almost
without preparatory drawing and in
patches of color, a technique which
allowed Guardi to achieve an
impressionistic effect.

CANALETTO
(Giovanni Antonio Canal)
(Venice 1697 - 1768)

The Dogana (Customs House) in Venice

Canvas, 46 x 63 cm
ca. 1735

The Venetian *vedute* paintings reached
their first high point with Canaletto's
works: His paintings were bought by
travelers from all over Europe,
particularly the English, as reminders of
the charm of Venice. Today they are to
be found in all large museums.

BERNARDO BELLOTTO
(known as Canaletto, Venice 1721 - Warsaw 1780)

Vienna from the Belvedere

canvas, 136 x 214 cm
1759/60

The Freyung in Vienna, from the Southeast

canvas, 116 x 152 cm
1758/61

Bellotto, nephew and pupil of Canaletto, also inherited his nickname. After a brief period of work in Northern Italy he was active in Dresden from 1747 to 1758 and when the city was destroyed by Prussian bombs during the Seven Years War, he went to Vienna where he painted numerous views for Empress Maria Theresa and the high nobility. The Vienna Gallery has thirteen of his paintings, views of Schloss Schönbrunn and of the Hofburg, as well as of the most important squares and buildings, modern at the time, in the city.

THE EGYPTIAN AND NEAR EASTERN COLLECTION

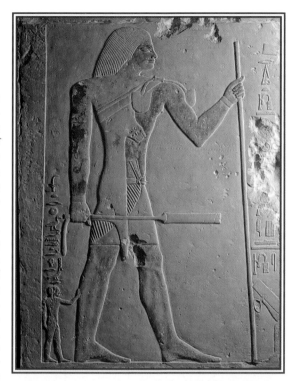

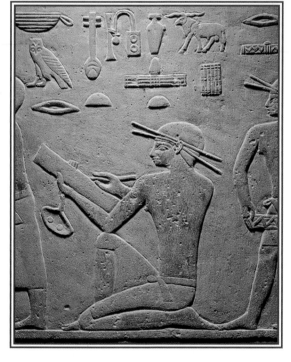

*T*he Egyptian collection in the Kunsthistorisches Museum is not only one of the largest of its kind, but also one of the oldest. The collection already had a basic stock before European interest in Egypt was stimulated by Napoleon's expedition of 1798. By the first quarter of the 19th century, the inventory had increased to almost 4000 pieces. One of the first documented objects in the collection - a statue from the Late Period - was acquired as early as the 16th century. The collection was considerably enlarged in 1878 by the acquisition of the Miramar collection, which had been assembled by Archduke Ferdinand Max (Emperor Maximilian of Mexico). In the 20th century, Austrian excavations in Egypt were the most important source for new additions, especially the digs in the necropolis of the Cheops pyramid carried out between 1912 and 1929. The new excavations brought as their share of the finds a great deal of material which is significant from a cultural and historical point of view.

The collection is most important for its fine sculpture from all periods of Pharaonic times, especially the Old Kingdom (3rd millennium B.C.). However all other sectors are also well represented (reliefs, architectural elements, minor sculpture in stone, bronze, wood, etc., sarcophagi and objects from the cult of the dead, papyri, scarabs, amulets, and jewelry as well as other significant documents of Egyptian culture).

The exhibition halls of the Egyptian collection are in an Egyptian style, typical of the period in which they were designed, and incorporate three original granite columns (monoliths about 7 meters high, dating to ca. 1420 B.C.). The wall paintings, by the pioneer of archaeological drawing, Ernst Weidenbach, reproduce the lively and informative interior decoration of the funeral chamber of an early prince.

Relief from the tomb of Prince Kaninisut in Giza

Old Kingdom, 5th Dynasty,
ca. 2400

These reliefs are from the cult chamber of the Prince's mastaba tomb. These chambers in the 5th-century tombs were used for the private cult of the dead. The pictures shown in the limestone reliefs deal with the care of the dead with food and drink and tell us about the family and the life style of the deceased. The reliefs to be seen here show Kaninisut, who was an influential man at the court of the king, and one of his scribes.

Head of a man, so-called "reserve head", from Giza

Old Kingdom, mid-4th Dynasty, ca. 2550
limestone, ht. 27.7 cm

Numerous life-size portrait heads were found in the Old Kingdom tombs or mortuary chambers, underground. These striking heads, which are not fragments of statues, probably had a magical significance, once attributed to all portraits. Their extraordinary artistic effectiveness served to preserve the memory of the appearance of the deceased.

Model of a boat

Middle Kingdom, probably 12th Dynasty, ca. 1950
painted wood, length ca. 55 cm

Models of boats were among the objects included in the tomb and they too were meant to allow the deceased to lead a normal life in the hereafter. The boat shown was a luxurious passenger boat, with prow and stern in the form of lotus flowers.

Statue of Sebekemsaf, from Armant

Middle Kingdom, 13th Dynasty, ca. 1700
black diorite, ht. 150 cm.

The imposing statue of this illustrious governor, who bore the
title "Orator of Thebes", is a mercilessly realistic work which
also stressed the dignity of the man who stands before his lord
and god. Inscriptions on his skirt tell us the name and origins
of the personage.

Statue of Sneferunofer, from Giza

Old Kingdom, 5th Dynasty, ca. 2400
limestone with traces of painting, ht. 78 cm

The man portrayed was the head singer at the court of the
pharaoh and director of music performances and other
entertainments on festive occasions; one of his tasks was also
that of composing music and poetry. This fine statue is an
excellent example of the linearity and formal symmetry of
early Egyptian sculpture. One can even visualize the square
form of the block from which the artist drew forth the figure.

Head of the pharaoh Sesostris III

Middle Kingdom, 12th Dynasty,
ca. 1850
green slate, ht. ca. 22 cm

The striped cloth with the figure of a
Uraeus serpent at the top tells us that
this head is that of a king. The features
identify him as the powerful Sesostris
III. The work was probably a fragment
of a king-sphinx, and was therefore
originally joined to a lion-shaped body.

Statue of King Thutmosis III

New Kingdom, 18th Dynasty,
ca. 1450
Black granite, ht. 46.5 cm

One of the finest heads of an Egyptian
king. The material has been worked with
extraordinary care and with great
expressive power.

Head of the statue of King Amenemhet V

Middle Kingdom, 13th Dynasty, ca. 1760
green slate, ht. 35 cm

The delicacy and elegance of the features are
closer to the artistic production of the New
Kingdom.

Book of the Dead of Chonsu-mes of Thebes (two details)

Third Intermediate Period, 21st Dynasty, ca. 1000
papyrus, overall length 420 cm

Chonsu-mes (also Chensu-mose) was an official of the treasury
chamber of the Temple of Amun in Thebes, superintendent of
the goldsmith workshops and temple building. The books of
the dead were papyrus scrolls which accompanied the dead into
the tomb. They contained ritual maxims, words that were to
serve for the well being of the deceased in the hereafter and
pictures with the description of mythological scenes. Shown
here are two illustrations from the book of the dead: above, that
of the deceased praying to the West (realm of the dead, falcon
and ostrich feather) and to the Ram, "the great god in his sun";
below, the court of the dead before Osiris, where the heart of
the deceased is set on one of the plates of the scales. His guide
is the jackal-headed god, Anubis.

Ushabti (Shawabti) figurines

various periods
blue, green and yellow faience

Chest for objects of the mortuary cult, from Thebes

21st Dynasty, 11th/10th cent.
painted wood, ht. 34 cm

Ushabtis or shawabtis were figurines to serve both as servants
and as substitutes of the deceased in the realm of the dead.
They are marked with the name of the deceased and were often
kept in boxes such as the one shown here. Left: Ushabti of Es-
chon, Third Intermediary Period, 21st Dynasty, ca. 950. At the
center, Ushabti of a priest of Memphis named Tji-har-pto, 30th
Dynasty, ca. 350 (see also adjacent photo). Right, Ushabti of
King Psammetich of the Late Period, ca. 600.

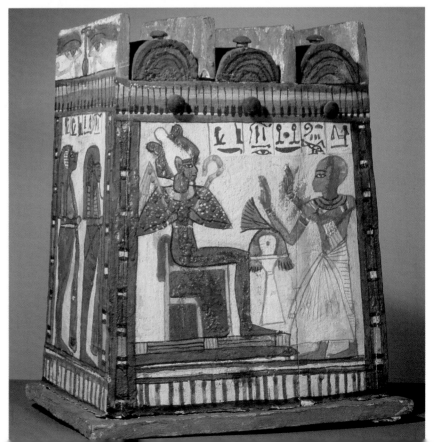

Standing hippopotamus

Middle Kingdom, ca. 2000
blue faience, length 20.5 cm

At the time of the Middle Kingdom, the mighty hippopotamus, a religious symbol and therefore often also object of a funerary cult, lived only in the southern part of the valley of the Nile. Lotus flowers and a wild duck, alluding to his habitat, as well as the eyes and teeth, are painted on this finely modelled hippo.

Unguent vase in the shape of a monkey with its young

Old Kingdom, 6th Dynasty, ca. 2260
alabaster, ht. 14.4 cm

The unguent vase bears the name of King Pepi I; it may have been a regal gift.

Portrait of a lady, sculptor's working model

New Kingdom, 19th Dynasty, ca. 1300
limestone, ht. 22.6 cm

The features of the lady and her full wig are delineated with a subtle delicacy. An open lotus flower is carved on her forehead.

◄ **Head of a ram**

New Kingdom, approximately 19th Dynasty, ca. 1250
black steatite

This is a votive offering to Amon.

Falcon, sculptor's working model

Ptolemaic period, ca. 3rd cent. B.C.
limestone

The refined treatment of the plumage is particularly admirable here, an example of the attention to detail apparent in so many of the animals shown in Egyptian art. Working models and examples used in teaching have come to light in sculptors' workshops, mostly dating to the period of the New Kingdom, found in the course of excavations.

Lion killing a calf

Late Period, probably 30th Dynasty, 4th cent. B.C.
green slate, length 61.5 cm

This piece of sculpture, undoubtedly a cult object, shows the beast sinking his fangs into the neck of the calf. A work of art of high quality.

Statuette of a queen or goddess

Ptolemaic, ca. 3rd cent. B.C.
black granite, ht. 65.5 cm

The slender long-limbed figure is an excellent example of the ideal female body, which one might say was manneristic, in the Ptolemaic period. The finely finished torso bears no inscription, so the subject and the date of the work remain uncertain.

Head of an old man ▶

Ptolemaic, 3rd cent. B.C.
green slate, ht. 31.3 cm

This excellent sculpture is a fragment of a life-size statue. The sense of realism and life in this portrait of an old man bears witness to the importance of Hellenistic art. But the underlying definition of the figure, the symmetry, are still unequivocably Egyptian.

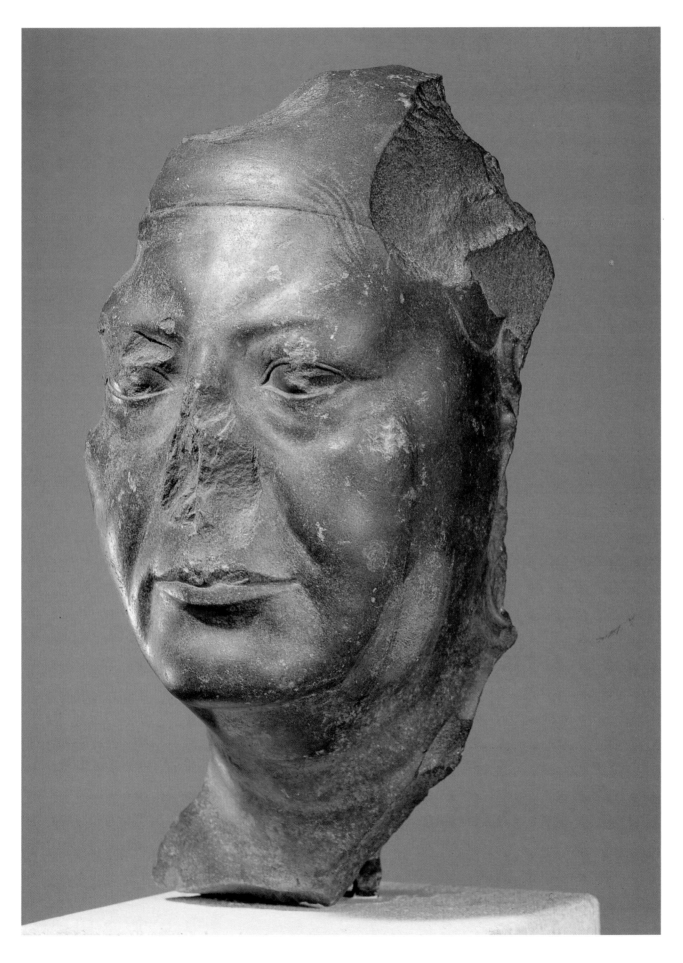

*Room X of the Antique Collection, in the post World War II
installation. At the center, the Youth of Magdalensberg, 16th
century copy of a Roman original. On the left, the Amazon
Sarcophagus, the head of Aristotle (cfr. p. 94) and the
colossal head of Athena.*

*T*he Collection of Greek, Etruscan and Roman Antiquities, together with treasure finds from the times of the Barbarian Migrations and the Early Middle Ages, is the largest part of the museum and is also connected with the Museum of Ephesos in the Neue Hofburg.

Ever since the 16th century, antiques have been collected at the Vienna court. The preference was for small objects such as coins, engraved stones, and bronzes. The foundations for the present-day collection were laid at the end of the 18th century with the unification of the imperial collections of antiquities, and the arrival of archaeological finds from all parts of the great kingdom, and the purchase of private collections. Austrian-sponsored archaeological research in the Eastern Greek area of civilization (Samothrace 1873/75, Gölbaşi-Trysa 1882/84, and Ephesos 1896/1906)

resulted above all in an increase in the number of objects in the field of sculpture and architecture. When antiquities from the then "Österreichisches Museum für Kunst und Industrie" were transferred in 1940, priceless pieces were added to the collection of Greek vases. One of the focal points of the Vienna antique collections is the unique group of cameos (remarkable masterpieces of Hellenistic and Roman glyptics: the Ptolemy Cameo, Gemma Augustea, Eagle Cameo). Others are outstanding examples of ancient sculture (Youth from Magdalensberg, bronze athlete from Ephesos, Amazon Sarcophagus, portrait of Aristotle, relief from the Parthian monument in Ephesos) and Greek pottery (cups by Douris, skyphos by the Brygos Painter) as well as gold and silver treasures from the period of the Barbarian Migrations (grave of a woman from Untersiebenbrunn) and the early Middle Ages (gold treasure from Nagyszentmiklós).

Polychrome white-ground lekythos

Attic, 2nd half 5th cent. B.C.
painted terra cotta, ht. 48.6 cm

With bent head, a youth, shown on the steps of his funeral stele, plays the lyre with his left hand. The young woman on the left, in sign of mourning, is clothed in black, with her disheveled hair cut short.

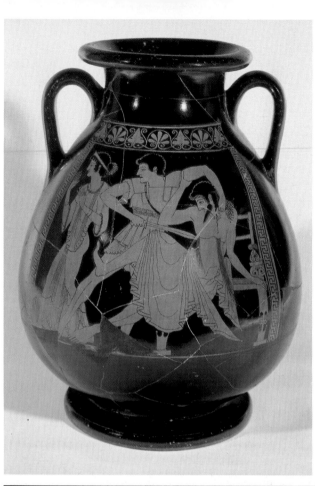

Pelike (recipient for food)

Attic, ca. 500 B.C.
terra cotta, red-figured, ht. 35 cm

As ordered by the god Apollo, Orestes, son of Agamemnon and Clitemnestra, takes bloody revenge on Aegisthus, who murdered his father and was his mother's lover.

Red-figured skyphos

Attic, by the Brygos Painter, ca. 490 B.C.
terra cotta, red-figured, ht. 25 cm

The skyphos, a large cup-shaped drinking bowl, shows the Trojan king Priam as he approaches the Greek hero Achilles to ask him to return the body of his dead son, Hector.

Small marble head of the goddess Artemis ▶

Hellenistic, 3rd to 1st cent. B.C.
marble, ht. 29 cm

This charming head, made to be set into a statue, was found in Tralles, in Asia Minor.

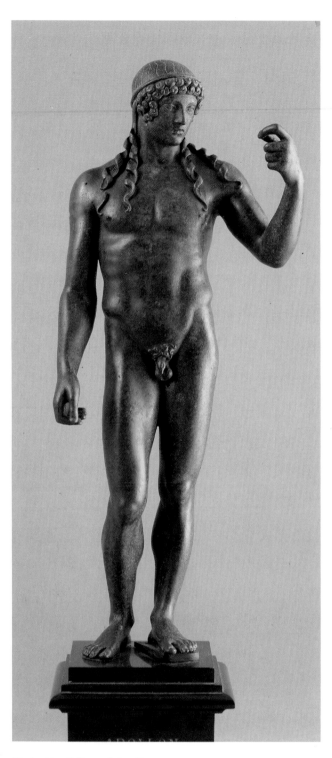

Statuette of the god Apollo

Greek, 1st cent. B.C.
bronze, ht. 28.5 cm

Statuette of the hero Herakles

Greek, 4th cent B.C.
bronze, ht. 33.2 cm

Apollo appears as the god who wards off illness: he held a bow
in his right hand and a laurel branch in his left. Herakles has a
lion skin thrown over his shoulder and, originally, probably
held a club, bow and arrow.

Half-figure of a centaur

Greek, 2nd cent. B.C.
silver, ht. 22 cm

This masterpiece by a Hellenistic silversmith was found near
Civita Castellana, the ancient Falerii. The piece is hollow cast
and consists of several parts. It may originally have been the
handle of a drinking horn.

Head of the philosopher Aristotle
(384-322 B.C.)

Roman copy of a Greek original of the 4th cent.B.C.
marble, ht. 30.5 cm

This great European philosopher, originally from Macedonia and a disciple of Plato, was also famous as the tutor of Alexander the Great. This piece is an example of the new art of portraiture, interested, at the beginning of the Hellenistic period, in depicting the individual forms.

Amazon Sarcophagus

Greek, 2nd half of the 4th cent B.C.
marble, length 216 cm

This famous work, discovered in Cyprus in the 16th century, is also known as the *Fugger Sarcophagus* after its first owners, rich merchants from Augsburg. This picture shows the central part of the composition: a Greek tries to help up a fallen companion and protect him from the blow of an Amazon axe; on the right, a Greek throws another Amazon from her horse.

Statuette of the goddess Artemis

Greek, 2nd cent B.C.
marble, ht. 78 cm

Frequently this statuette is known by the name of its site of discovery, present-day Lanarca on the island of Cyprus. The goddess, dressed in the classic chiton, lazily leans on the classical statuette dedicated to her. In her right hand she probably held a torch and perhaps, in her left, a bow. The artist who executed this figure was still under the influence of the great art of Praxiteles.

Gemma Augustea

Roman, around the birth of Christ
two-layered onyx, ht. 19 cm

This cameo, which originally belonged
to the Emperor Augustus, was cut from
an onyx with white and dark brown
layers. The upper part shows the
triumphant Tiberius before his stepfather
Augustus and Roma, goddess of the city;
in the lower tier, Roman legionaries
raise their victory trophy. This splendid
work of art was made to celebrate the
repression of a Dalmatian insurrection
by Tiberius in 9 B.C.

Eagle Cameo

Roman, 27 B.C.
multi-layered onyx, Italian setting,
late 16th cent.
diam. 22 cm

The eagle of Roman victory with the
oak garland and a palm frond refers to
the conferral of the *corona civica* on the
Emperor Augustus in 27 B.C. for having
brought the civil war to an end.

Ptolemy Cameo

Greco-Hellenistic, 274-270 B.C.
nine-layered onyx, ht. 11.5 cm

This cameo with its portraits of a royal Ptolemaic couple is
generally considered a masterpiece of Greek glyptic art.
Ancient techniques have been masterfully employed in using
the alternately light and dark layers of onyx to depict both
figures. Probably they are the royal Egyptian couple,
Ptolemy II and Arsinoe II.

Portrait of a lady: Fayum mummy portrait

Egyptian-Roman, 3rd cent. A.D.
encaustic painting on wood, ht. 36.9 cm

In Roman times the practice developed in Egypt of covering the face of the mummy with a painted portrait, a custom which fell into disuse when Christianity prevailed. The lady, shown in a pink dress, wears rich jewels and her hair is fashionably coiffed. The mummy portraits are of particular importance in the history of culture for they are better preserved than any other type of painted portrait.

Bust of Eutropios

Early Byzantine period, 2nd half 5th cent. A.D.
marble, ht. 32 cm

This bust, of a citizen named Eutropios, was found during the
Austrian excavations at Ephesos. The influence of Christianity
comes to the fore in this work of great quality: indeed what
matters in this portrait is no longer the quest for classical
beauty but the search for a greater spiritual expression.

Two gala fibulas, from the tomb of Untersiebenbrunn

Germanic, early 5th cent. A.D.
gold, silver, with mounted stones,
length ca. 16 cm

These two fibulas were part of the most important excavation treasure dating to the period of the migrations in Austria. Found in 1910 in the rich tomb of a Germanic princess, in Untersiebenbrunn (Lower Austria), they are sown with colored stones (principally almandines), vitreous paste and green enamel. The core of the mounting is silver, with a gold leaf covering, decorated with granulation and filigree. At the beginning of the 5th century, the goldwork of the Germanic tribes was the fruit of an age-old development with various influences. The technique of granulation and filigree decoration came from the area of the Mediterranean, while they had learned how to combine glittering gold with colored stones from their contacts with the Scythians, in the territory of the Black Sea.

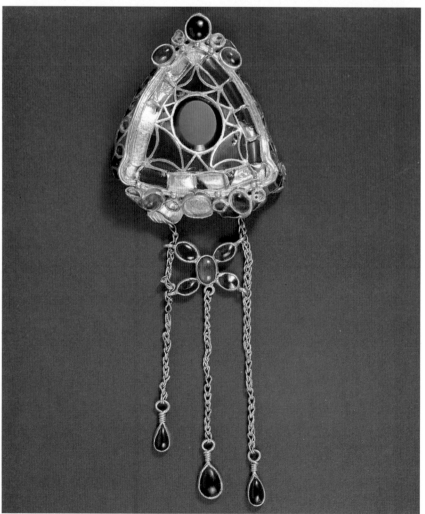

Gala fibula from Nagymihály

Germanic, 2nd half of the 4th cent. A.D.
gold with mounted stones,
length 19.5 cm

This splendid gold fibula set with stones and three pendant chains was found in Rebrin, in Slovacchia, in 1852. This region at the time belonged to the Hungarians so the fibula came to be known by the name of the principal Hungarian site. It is a magnificent example of the polychrome decorative style (contrast between stones and gold) of Germanic goldwork.

Gold treasure of Nagyszentmiklós

The gold treasure, found in 1799 in Nagyszentmiklós (now Sinicolaul Mare, Romania), consists of 23 gold vessels which altogether weigh almost ten kilos. This unique early medieval treasure trove is probably the product of old Bulgarian art of the 9th century A.D. and is a mixture of various stylistic influences: central Asian, Persian-Sassanian characteristics are found side by side with Hellenistic-Roman and Byzantine features, pagan next to purely Christian ones.

Medallion vase: armed rider with a bannered spear, who holds a prisoner by his topknot; a human head is on his saddle.

Ancient Bulgarian,
2nd half of the 9th cent. A.D.
gold, 18 carats, ht. 22 cm, weight g 608

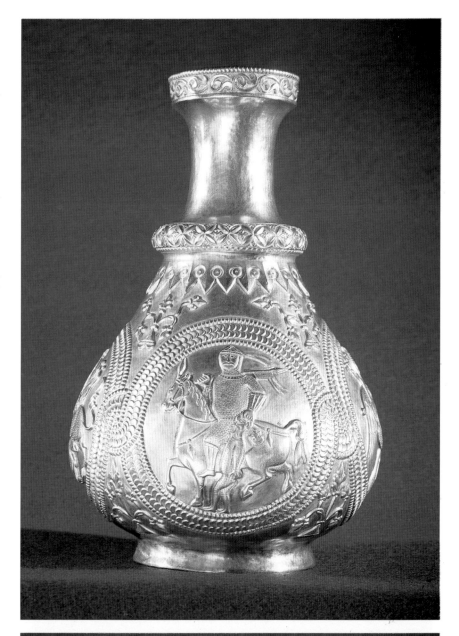

Bull's head cup: supported by three of the animal's legs and decorated with plant motifs.

Ancient Bulgarian,
2nd half of 9th cent. A.D.
gold, 20 carats, length 17.7 cm,
weight g 283

Two reliefs from a fountain

Sheep and lamb
Lioness with two cubs

Roman art, first half 1st cent A.D.
found at Praeneste (Palestrina),
near Rome
marble, ht. respectively 96 and 94 cm

Both scenes take place in a natural landscape but in the vicinity of man: in the background of the panel with the sheep we see a temple-shaped building and a shepherd's bundle hangs from the oak. Above the lion's den is a small aedicule to Dionysus, the god of wine and fertility.

Consular diptych
Personifications of the two ancient metropolitan cities of Rome (left) **and Constantinople**

Western Roman art,
2nd half 5th cent. A.D.
ivory, ht. 27.4 cm

The diptychs were originally small waxed tablets for taking notes which could then be wiped out, whenever required. They took their names from the two consuls, the highest officials in Republican Rome, elected, each time, for a year. The artistic execution in ivory, an extremely rare material in antiquity, indicates that this was not simply an object of use.

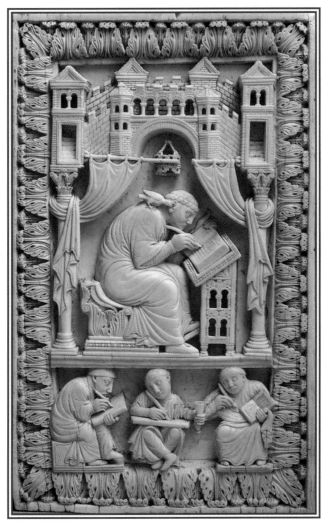

*T*he pieces in this collection are a direct continuation in time of the early medieval objects in the Antikensammlung and cover the period from the Middle Ages through the Renaissance, the Baroque and the Rococo up to the early 19th century. The collection centers around the material collected in the 16th and 17th centuries, as is true of the Picture Gallery, which was the period of great Hapsburg collectors and patrons. The most important sectors include examples of the goldsmith's art, glyptics, bronzes, carved and turned ivory, as well as tapestries. The objects from the Renaissance Kunst- und Wunderkammern ("Art and Marvel Cabinets") are exceptional in execution or what they represent.

The artists of the Middle Ages worked almost exclusively for churches and monasteries, and even what was commissioned by secular princes served a religious purpose. This does not mean that antiquity and its art were forgotten, but simply that the significance changed. The ivory tablet with St. Gregory and three scribes is in the antique tradition of the consular diptychs. Such ivory panels were used as decoration on book covers and were preserved in the treasuries of monasteries or cathedrals. The tablet with St. Gregory was already in Leopold William's Kunstkammer in 1647. While only a few examples of medieval art are to be found in the collection of sculpture and applied arts, they are particularly significant. The most impor-

tant group is the treasure of the Germanic queens and emperors of the Middle Ages, the so-called imperial treasure, which is on exhibit in the Hofburg as part of the secular Schatzkammer or treasure cabinet. The sacred character of medieval art is particularly evident in the pieces in this treasure. Nevertheless the artists of the Middle Ages, such as goldsmiths and enamelers, reverted to the most curious themes of ancient, Near Eastern, or Germanic mythology. The aquamanile in the shape of a griffin exemplifies this tradition. The fabulous animal becomes a symbolic figure for Christ, who by his death freed man from sin, just as the water which is poured out of the pitcher cleanses the hands of the priest. Medieval religious art finds its loveliest expression in the representations of the Madonna and Child. The Kunsthistorisches Museum owns two magnificent works of this kind. The Madonna from the south Bohemian city of Krumau is considered a particularly fine example of the so-called International Gothic style, which characterized all of Europe around 1400. These works have been called the "Beautiful Madonnas" (Schöne Madonnen) because of their sweet expression, the elegant figure, and the artful draping of the clothes. The wood sculpture by Tilman Riemenschneider dates from the last phase of the German Late Gothic and still has its original color.

Saint Gregory and three scribes

Carolingian (Lotharingian?), ca. 980
ivory, ht. 20.5 cm

This relief was originally the central part of the outer covering of a book. It shows St. Gregory the Great, pope from 590 to 604. He was listed among the Latin Fathers of the church because, a descendent of senatorial nobility, he was an authoritative mediator between the early Christian and the medieval culture of the West, both in the field of theology and in the practice of the Christian life.

The Krumau Madonna

Bohemian (Prague?), ca. 1400
limestone with traces of the original painting, ht. 112 cm

A type of Madonna that developed in the late 14th century under the influence of the art of the court of Prague is known as the "Schöne Madonna". One of the loveliest and sweetest comes from the city of Krumau, in southern Bohemia.

◄ **Aquamanile in the shape of a griffin**

Lotharingian, 2nd half 12th cent.
bronze with gilding, simulated, in part, with silvering,
ht. 17 cm

The aquamanile was used in the liturgical washing of the hands at the beginning of the holy mass, a purely symbolic act. Numerous mythical animals, such as the unicorn and the griffin, were symbols of Christ in the Middle Ages.
The concept at the base of this object is as follows: as the water poured from the griffin-pitcher purifies the hands, thus Christ purifies the soul.

TILMAN RIEMENSCHNEIDER
(Osterode 1460 - Würzburg 1531)

Madonna and Child

ca. 1500
linden wood, ht. 145 cm

Riemenschneider's figures are the expressions of an elevated concept of the meaning of religious art. His sculpture is an invitation to give oneself up to the contemplation of faith, a call facilitated by the universal validity of the work of art.

Samples of a traveling salesman

Bohemian or Austrian, ca. 1400
all in all 56 colored drawings on paper
applied to maple wood, each 9.5 x 9 cm

Like other types of workers, painters too moved from one place
to another and employed collections of models of religious or
secular motifs in soliciting commissions. An example, with a
particularly wide range of well executed pieces, is the so-called
Viennese Sampler which must have been made in an art center,
such as Prague or Vienna, where various currents of the time
converged.

Playing cards with the game of court appointments

Austrian (Vienna?), ca. 1450
paper, woodcut, painting with gold and silver leaf,
ca. 14 x 10 cm

The set includes 48 cards in a perfect state of preservation. The cards are subdivided into four series, which are distinguished by the coats of arms of the kingdoms of Bohemia, Germany, France and Hungary. Each region had its court, its official (administrative) representative, servants and craftsmen. The cards shown above include a messenger, an archer, a cook, the Hungarian king, a potter and a German queen.

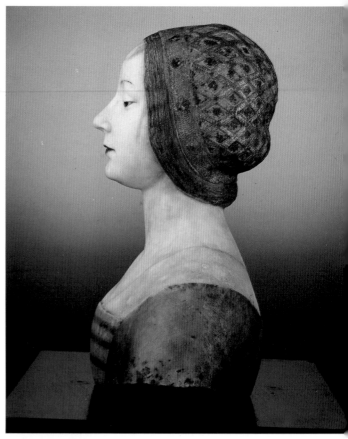

DESIDERIO DA SETTIGNANO
(Florence 1430 - 1464)

Laughing Boy

ca. 1455
marble bust, ht. 33 cm

Following in the footsteps of Donatello and Luca della Robbia, Desiderio often delighted in depicting children and here he has succeeded in giving his subject an extremely natural and amiable expression.

FRANCESCO LAURANA
(Vrana in Dalmatia ca. 1430 - in France 1502)

**Portrait of Isabella of Aragon
Princess of Naples**

ca. 1488
polychrome marble, ht. ca. 44 cm

Laurana was one of the great artists of the Italian Renaissance who traveled widely. He sojourned in Naples more than once, where he made busts of the royal princesses. Isabella later married the duke of Milan. The splendid work is characterized by a mixture of virginal shyness and haughty aloofness.

Entombment of Christ

North Italian, ca. 1480
bronze, partially gilt,
ht. 24.3 cm

The relief is effective thanks to the intense expression of grief and the perfect modeling of the figures. The unknown artist was undoubtedly influenced by Donatello.

ANTONIO ROSSELLINO
(Florence 1427 - 1479)

Madonna and Child

ca. 1465
marble relief, ht. 69.5 cm

There is something very private in the
way in which the Florentine sculptors
and painters depicted the young mother
with her divine son, in perfect keeping
with the sense of intimacy that
accompanied the worship of Mary at the
time.

TULLIO LOMBARDO
(Venice ca. 1455 - 1532)

Bacchus and Ariadne

ca. 1505
marble relief, ht. 55 cm

More than most other North Italian
works, this splendid relief links up to
ancient Roman sculpture. Bacchus and
Ariadne, the classical couple of ancient
mythology, are shown with great
sensitivity. Compare in this sense the
work by Antico, show on the following
page.

ANTICO
(Pier Jacopo Alari Buonacolsi)
(Mantua ca. 1460 - Gazzuolo 1528)

Bacchus and Ariadne

Mantua, ca. 1520/25
partially gilt bronze,
ht. respectively 59 and 50 cm

Bacchus is identified by the bunches of
grapes and tendrils in his hair, while the
branches of hops on the head of Ariadne
are a symbol of sleep, from which
Bacchus awakened her. The relationship
between these two personages in this
work by Antico is not based so much on
love as it is on an idea of classic
harmony.

◀ BERTOLDO DI GIOVANNI

(Florence ca.1420 - Poggio a Caiano 1491)

Bellerophon Tames Pegasus

Florence, ca. 1480
bronze, ht. 32.5 cm

This statuette is one of the most significant works realized in
the technique of bronze casting. Bertoldo was a pupil of
Donatello and Michelangelo's teacher. The figure shown here
is Bellerophon who succeeded in taming Pegasus, the winged
horse of Zeus. He then accomplished numerous heroic deeds
with Pegasus as his mount.

Two bird-shaped vessels

Saracchi workshop
Milan, late 16th cent.
rock crystal mounted in gold, with precious stones and pearls,
ht. respectively 41 and 23 cm

The Saracchi were an important family of engravers of pietre
dure in Milan. These recipients in imaginative shapes were
called "Reiger" (cranes) in the old inventories. The surface of
the crystal is completely covered with wheel-engraved motifs.

GREGOR ERHART
(Ulm ca. 1468 - Augsburg 1540)

Allegory of Vanity (The Ephemeral)

Augsburg, ca. 1500
linden wood with the original painting,
ht. 46 cm

This work of art wants to remind the
observer of the transience of youth and
beauty. Contacts between medieval
thought and the renewed interest in the
repertory of images of classic antiquity
are already apparent.

ANDREA RICCIO
(Trento? ca. 1470 - Padua 1532)

Seated Satyr

ca. 1520
bronze, ht. 21.7 cm

Boy with Goose

ca. 1515
bronze, ht. 19.6 cm

Both statues are captivating in the naturalness of the movement and the vivacity of expression.

CHRISTOPH WEIDITZ
(Augsburg ca. 1500 - 1559)

Adam and Eve

ca. 1540
pear, ht. 32 cm

In their notably slender proportions and studied gestures these statuettes do not seem to be works by Weiditz, but later pieces under the influence of Mannerism, even though the problem of their attribution still remains an open question.

"Dürerpokal"

Nürnberg, ca. 1500
gilded silver, ht. 47.8 cm

This pokal or cup with cover has been associated with the great painter Albrecht Dürer who learned the art of goldwork in his youth. Among his drawings and sketches, designs for artistic cups with the characteristic curves to be seen in this work frequently appear.

Double cup in rock crystal

Nürnberg, 2nd half 15th cent.
rock crystal, mounting in gilded silver, ht. 24.5 cm

Rock crystals of exceptional purity were as prized as gold and silver and were used to create these luxurious drinking vessels. The two cups of different size, seen in this picture one on top of the other, were probably used when toasts were drunk by the guest and the host, woman and man.

"Michael Beaker"

France, ca. 1530/40
gold studded with diamonds, rubies,
emeralds and pearls,
ht. 52 cm

This sumptuous beaker or pokal was a
gift from King Charles IX of France to
Archduke Ferdinand II of Austria. It is
one of the few extant masterworks of
French Renaissance goldwork.

Vessel and cup with dragon

Florence, ca. 1580
lapis lazuli, gold with enamel,
ht. respectively, 36 and 17 cm

ALESSANDRO VITTORIA
(Trento 1525 - Venice 1608)

Noble Venetian Lady

Venice, ca. 1570
terra cotta, ht. 83 cm

This expressive bust comes from the Palazzo Zorzi in Venice. A mental comparison of this masterpiece by Alessandro Vittoria with the contemporary portraits by Titian and Tintoretto gives us an idea of the high level attained by Venetian portraiture in this period.

GIAMBOLOGNA
(Jean de Boulogne)
(Douai 1529 - Florence 1608)

Walking Lion

bronze, ht. 13.5 cm

Astronomy

ca. 1573
fire gilt bronze, ht. 38.8 cm

**Group of two figures with the
abduction of a woman**

ca. 1579
bronze, ht. ca. 98 cm

Giambologna succeeded in composing
figures or groups of figures so that the
view from all sides was satisfactory. The
group of two figures communicates
particularly well the impression of
natural movement, even more so when
one moves around the piece to observe it.
The figure of Astronomy also turns in
a spiral movement, in what was known
as the *figura serpentinata*. The statuette
is signed by the artist and he himself
probably gave it to Emperor
Maximilian II.

Danae

French, 1541-1550
tapestry in wool and silk, with gold and silver threads 330 x 625 cm

This tapestry is one of a series of 6 pieces which constituted the wall decoration executed by Florentine artists to order for the king of France, Francis I, for the great gallery of his château of Fontainebleau.

Three figures of the Commedia dell'Arte

Venice (Murano), ca. 1600
glass, ht. ca. 20 cm

These figures represent a well-known personage of the extemporaneous Italian theater of the time, the "Captain", in his characteristic gestures.

◀ Leda and the Swan

Italian, 2nd half 16th cent.
chalcedony and gold, ht. 7.3 cm

This small masterpiece has also been attributed to Benvenuto Cellini.

◀ Diana shown as a Black Woman

Milan, 2nd half 16th cent.
jasper, a large pearl, gold and diamonds, ht. 6.1 cm

The portrait of Diana, goddess of the hunt, is a skillfully cut gem that was only later mounted in gold, perhaps in Prague, when it was acquired by the Emperor Matthias.

BENVENUTO CELLINI
(Florence 1500 - 1572)

Salt cellar

1540-1543
partially enameled gold, ebony,
ht. 26 cm

This extraordinary work was made by Cellini for King Francis I of France. It is, first of all, a precious piece of tableware, with a small ship for salt (sea salt) and a small temple for pepper; it is also however an allegory of the world, represented by the god of the Sea and the goddess of the Earth.

CHRISTOPH GANTNER

(? - Innsbruck 1605)

Tantalus

ca. 1580/90
terra cotta with colored glass enamel, ht. 27 cm

Christoph Gantner has left us a series of vases in amusing
shapes, which he made for Archduke Ferdinand II, regent of
the Tyrol. Tantalus was a Greek hero condemned by the gods
to everlasting hunger, surrounded by food he could not reach.
Gantner interpreted this myth in a popular humorous way.

**Sample of ore with the representation of Christ on the
Mount of Olives, and, below, scenes in the mine**

Bohemian, late 16th cent
ht. 65 cm

Works of this kind are found in the Cabinets of Art and
Marvels of princes. They were done on samples of rock from a
mine and decorated with figures. The base of the object is in
gilded silver.

MELCHIOR MAIR
(ca. 1565 - Augsburg 1613)

Automatic clock:
Diana Riding a Centaur

Augsburg, ca. 1605
partially gilded silver, precious stones, enamel,
ht. 39.5 cm

The clock mechanism is in the stomach of the centaur, while the wooden base contains an automatic mechanism which activates the movements of the heads of the persons and the dog so that the centaur lets fly his arrow. These unusual "show pieces" were used as entertainment in a drinking game: the guest in whose direction the arrow fell had to formulate the toast and empty his glass.

JEREMIAS METZKER
(active in Augsburg between 1555 and 1559)

Table clock

Augsburg, 1564
gilded bronze, ht. 30 cm

ADRIAEN DE FRIES
(The Hague ca. 1545 - Prague 1626)

Emperor Rudolf II

Prague, 1603
bronze, ht. 112 cm

JOST BÜRGI
(Lichtensteig near San Gallo 1552 - Kassel 1632)

Table clock

Prague, ca. 1625
gilded brass, silver and rock crystal, ht. 18.6 cm

This type of clock has several faces, one for the hours of the
day, for the length of the day and the night, for dawn and
sunset, as well as one with the calendar and the representations
of the Zodiac. Emperor Rudolf II was extremely interested both
in the workings of the astronomers and the clockmakers as well
as the skill of the goldsmiths.

Tableware from the Kunstkammer of Rudolf II, in rare, often exotic materials, artistically mounted by the most famous goldsmiths of the time.

ANTON SCHWEINBERGER
(Augsburg, mid 16th cent. - Prague 1603)

Gala pitcher made of a palm nut from the Seychelles
Prague, ca. 1600
palm nut from the Seychelles,
gilded silver, ht. 37.8 cm

OTTAVIO MISERONI
(? - Prague 1624)

Cup in moss agate
Prague, ca. 1600, ht. 17 cm

PAUL VAN VIANEN
(Utrecht ca. 1570 - Prague 1613)

Pitcher in golden brown jasper
Milan, ca. 1570, ht. 35.5 cm

JAN VERMEYEN
(Brussels ca. 1555 - Prague 1606)

Vase of narwhal tusk with lid
ht. 22 cm

The Battle of Kahlenberg and the Liberation of Vienna, September 12, 1683

tapestry in wool and silk, 450 x 560 cm

This is part of a series of 19 tapestries made in 1724/25 to celebrate the victory of Duke Charles V of Lorraine, by the Lorraine manufacture Malgrange on a design by Charles Herbel.

Riding Lesson of Louis XIII of France

tapestry in wool and silk, 410 x 380 cm

This is part of a series of 8 pieces, made in Brussels in the middle of the 17th century to a design by Jacob Jordaens. Neptune shows the king how to execute a *haute école* figure, the *ballottade*.

MATTHIAS STEINL

(1644 - Vienna 1727)

Emperor Leopold I (1658-1705) as Conqueror of the Turks

Vienna, 1693
ivory statuette on an ebony base,
ht. ca. 70 cm

The Emperor's horse rears up over a Turk and various implements of war under which a Gallic rooster hides, a sign that the French were defeated together with their Turkish allies.

JAKOB AUER

(Haiming, Tyrol 1646 - Landeck 1706)

Apollo and Daphne

Vienna, late 17th cent.
ivory, ht. 44 cm

Fury

Southern Germany, 2nd half 17th cent.
ivory, ht. 37.5 cm

PAUL STRUDEL
(Cles, Tyrol 1648 - Vienna 1708)

Bust of the Emperor Leopold I

marble, ht. 86 cm
1695

Leopold I, who became emperor after the sudden death of his older brother, reigned for almost half a century. With him the Hapsburg kingdom rose to great power.

JEAN BAPTISTE LEMOYNE
(Paris 1704 - 1778)

Bust of the Archduchess Marie Antoinette

marble, ht. 76.5 cm
1771

Marie Antoinette, the younger daughter of the Empress Maria Theresa born in 1755, married the future king of France, Louis XVI, when she was fifteen, going directly from her children's room in Vienna, almost bourgeois in style, to the splendid dissolute environment of the court of Versailles. This caused the Empress great worry, as revealed by her numerous letters full of advice to her daughter, whose beauty triumphed in court for a few years of excessive irresponsibility. By the time she regained her sense of responsibility it was too late but she faced prison and the guillotine with a strength of character that was worthy of her great mother.

CAMILLO RUSCONI
(Milan 1658 - Rome 1728)

Bust of Giulia Albani degli Abati Olivieri

marble bust from the funeral monument in the church of S. Domenico in Pesaro, ht. 96 cm
1719

126

ANTON MATTHIAS DOMANEK
(Vienna 1713 - 1779)

Breakfast service of the Empress Maria Theresa

Milk and coffee pots in gold with ebony handles. Chocolate cup in porcelain in a gold holder, on a golden saucer with a handle, coffee bowl with matching saucer in porcelain. Gold spoons. The milk pitcher is 23.4 cm high.

INDEX OF NAMES